WUNDERKAMMER

THIJS DEMEULEMEESTER

WUNDERKAMMER

An Exotic Journey through Time

LANNOO

TABLE OF CONTENTS

INTRODUCTION

This is a book about discovery, about curiosity and adventure, about exploration and new trade routes – and also about distant civilizations and their exotic flora and fauna. Especially it's a book about knowledge, both fabricated and proven. *Wunderkammer. An Exotic Journey through Time* is an intrepid quest, albeit on paper, for the wonderful and curious, the outlandish and the outré. A thrilling boy's – and girl's! – own story, for hunters and collectors. It's also for people with patience, because you don't acquire an entire collection of exotica overnight. A collection is built over a lifetime. And for eight centuries people have been collection-building with a single end in view – to impress their contemporaries with their knowledge or wealth.

Those collections of exotica showcase nature's best and most beautiful, from ostrich eggs to narwhal tusks. They also demonstrate what man can do with nature. He can, for instance, prepare, stuff and mount the skins of animals with such lifelike effect that it's impossible to separate nature from the work of his own hand. Organizing unknown flowers in a herbarium is another example. That's empiricism versus nature. Does a plant even exist if it's never been given a scientific name? What if a goldsmith transforms a rare shell into an elegant piece of tableware? Who is the ultimate artist then? And what if we drink from a gold-lidded nautilus shell standing on a golden foot? Are we then putting nature on a pedestal? Do we award the laurels to the inventiveness of creation? Or are we trying to emulate or even surpass nature with our human ingenuity and craftsmanship? That is the covert contest in this collection of exotica: who is the greatest artist of the universe: nature or man? Who imitates whom? And which is making a fool of the other?

<<<

The botanical prints from Robert John Thornton's 'The Temple of Flora' (1798-1807) look like exotic landscapes.

<<

Visitors in Levinus Vincent's natural history cabinet in Haarlem, Andries van Buysen (1706).

<

The Viktor Wynd Museum of Curiosities in London houses a twenty-first-century *Wunderkammer.*

>

Maria Sibylla Merian (1647-1717) was an unconventional naturalist and scientific illustrator who published a major work on the insects of Surinam.

J. Mulder Sculp

Surinaamsche Flamingo

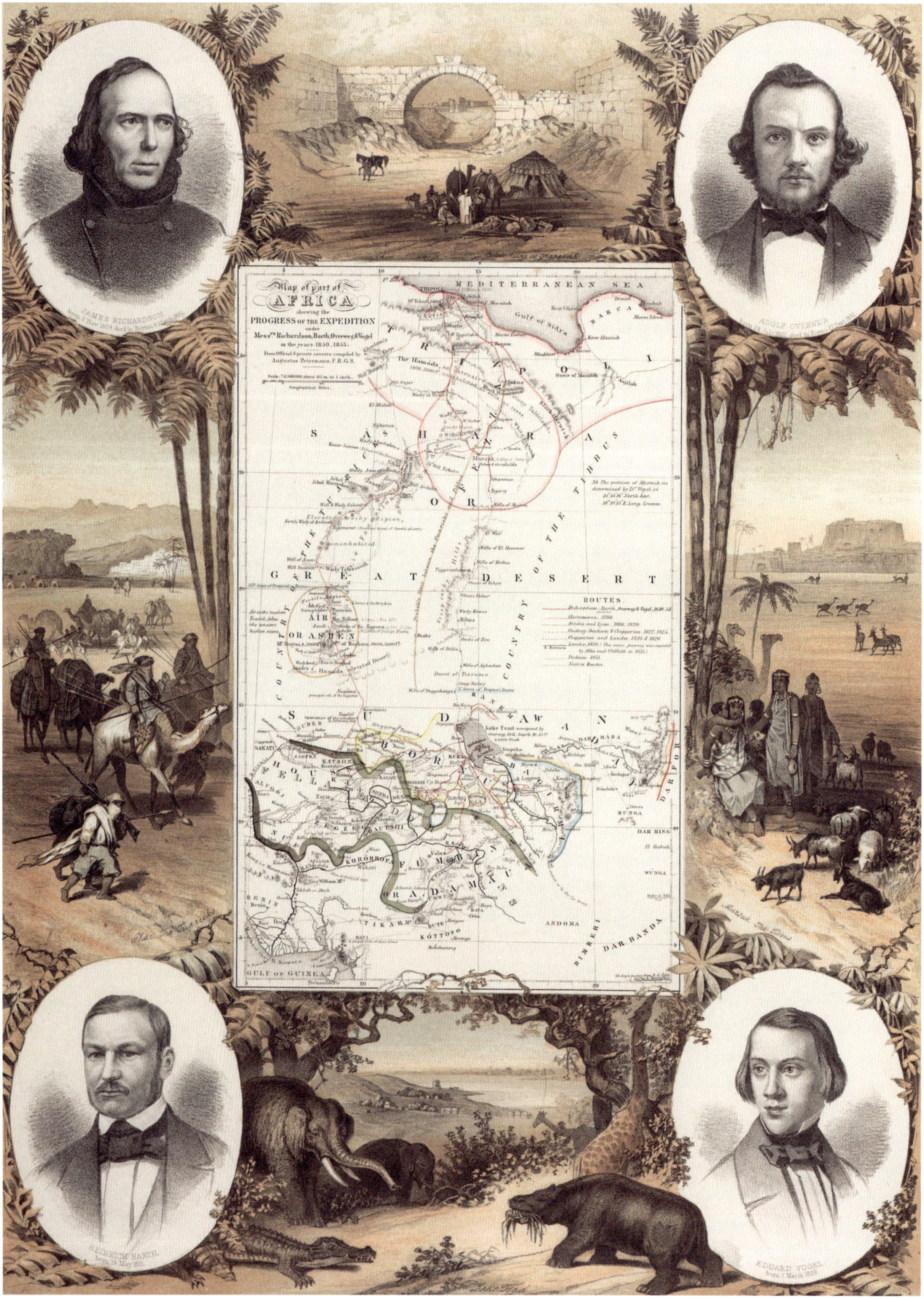
Map of part of
AFRICA
showing the
PROGRESS OF THE EXPEDITION
under
Mess.rs Richardson, Barth, Overweg & Vogel
in the years 1850_1855.
From Official & private sources compiled by
Augustus Petermann. F.R.G.S.
Geographical Miles
MEDITERRANEAN SEA
Gulf of Sidra
GREAT DESERT
ROUTES
GULF OF GUINEA
JAMES RICHARDSON
ADOLF OVERWEG
HEINRICH BARTH
born 16 May 1821.
EDUARD VOGEL
born 7 March 1829

Chapter 1

THE DISCOVERY OF CURIOSITY

From Medieval Bestiaries to Early Explorers:

How the Collecting of Exotica Began

—

Make sure your hands are clean.

Follow the guide obediently.

Don't admire things that aren't particularly rare.

You'll make yourself ridiculous.

after Casper F. Neickel, *Museographia*, 1727

—

Why does anyone collect exotica? At a guess, because nature has more imagination than man; because we're intrigued by the wonders of the natural world, particularly those things that are very rare or that we've never seen before. How else can we explain the popularity of television channels such as National Geographic and Discovery Channel? What are natural history programmes but exotica on film? For some, simply looking was not enough; collectors of exotica tried to improve on nature by arranging their specimens in a *Wunderkammer*, a 'chamber of wonders' or 'cabinet of curiosities'. Or they turned them into something more extraordinary still – a piece of ivory into an exquisite sculpture, a coconut into the support for a piece of virtuoso engraving …

<

This map of Central Africa, a title plate by F. Moras designed by August Heinrich Petermann, shows the European explorers James Richardson, Eduard Vogel, Heinrich Barth and Adolf Overweg who carried out an expedition to Central Africa from 1850 to 1853.

SLIPSTREAM

Man has been intrigued by fauna and flora for millennia. But the urge to collect them is more recent, and the desire to classify and organize specimens of the natural world that are strange and new to us is more recent still. That we put shells or rocks or holiday souvenirs on show in our living rooms today can be laid directly at the door of Vasco da Gama, James Cook, Christopher Columbus and all the less celebrated explorers who not only discovered new worlds but also the plants and animals that inhabited them. They came home full of travellers' tales that were eagerly lapped up by the less intrepid. Some of these stories were true, some were generously embellished, some were complete fabrications. But the result was the same: they inspired an unprecedented passion for exploration. The cabins of those bold adventurers were crammed with exotic and beguiling objects. No one had ever seen such things before. No one had ever studied them. No wonder that people at home were astonished by the extraordinary objects which the travellers brought back. Nor is it any wonder that canny merchants quickly spotted a market for all that exotic novelty. In the slipstream of their mercantile activity a maritime trade developed, a commerce in decorative items collectively known as exotica – from shells to minerals, from coconuts to ostrich eggs, from feathers to entire stuffed birds.

—

ENTER EXOTICA

In Europe collecting had begun in earnest in the Middle Ages. It was then that western nobles taking part in the first crusades encountered spices and other oriental products. Even before the first great voyages of discovery had set sail – journeys that would herald the end of the Middle Ages – merchants were travelling to Persia and India. By the thirteenth century you would have been able to find prestigious treasuries whose contents included exotica. But it was in the late fifteenth and early sixteenth centuries that the *Wunderkammer* really became an essential cultural appurtenance, especially for princes, prelates and the contemporary intelligentsia. The concept of collecting as an expression of the changing worldview was then relatively new. Renaissance humanists saw it as a way of bringing the world within grasp – in both senses of the word. And it was necessary to have a good grasp of the latest geographical news, for in that period the known world expanded with every voyage of exploration, as new and exotic lands were discovered. As those lands were claimed for the crown that had sponsored the explorers who found them, Europe's omnipotence as the only civilization was gradually revised. At the same time, the knowledge that those new parts of the world existed aroused all men's mercantile instincts. On a small scale this led to exotica in the *Wunderkammer*; on a large scale it led to colonization.

>

The first fleet of the second Portuguese expedition to India, led by Vasco da Gama in 1502, in the *Livro das Armadas*.

No Anno de 508.

Partirão pera a Jndia a cinq° e anove dabril /17/ Vellas Repartidas em duas capitanias móres .ss. Jorje da guiar por capitão mór de /13/ oyto pera a carga despeciaria, e cimquo pera elle com ellas fiqar darmada na costa darabia, e das quatro mays hia por capitão mor diogo lopez de sequeyra pera co ellas passar ao descobrimento de Mallaq.ª onde dis cobrindoa avia de fiqar co ho mesmo titullo de capitão mor /. e os capitães de todas erão os ss

Pera ho descobrimento de Mallaq.ª /.

Pera a carga despiciaria estas

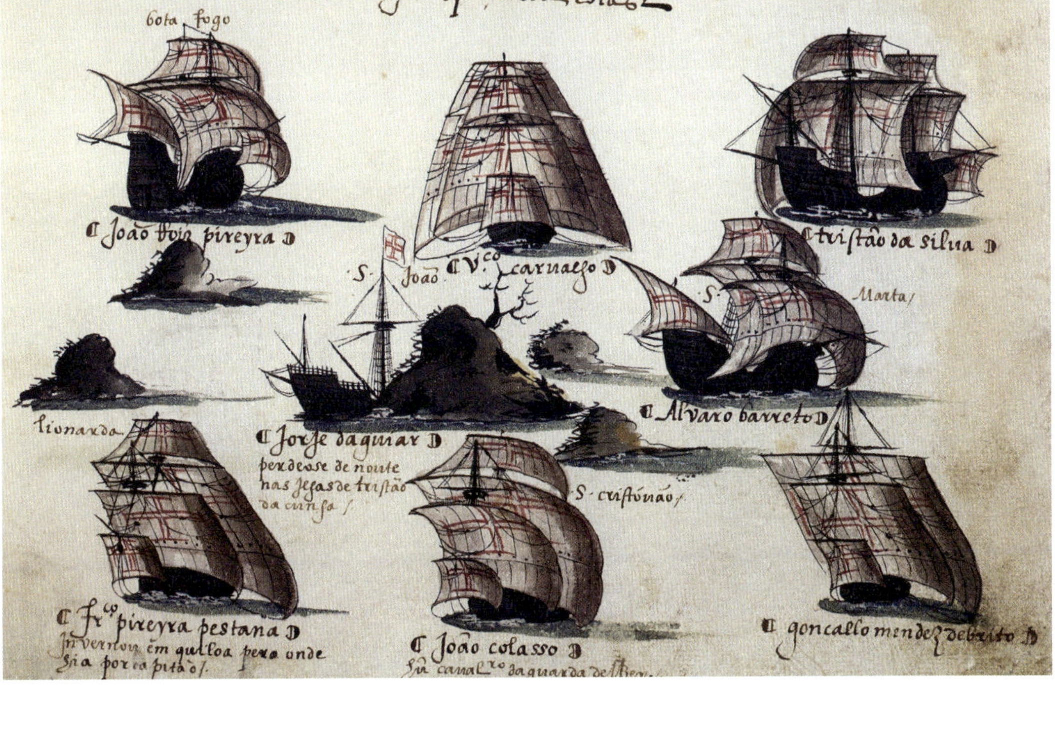

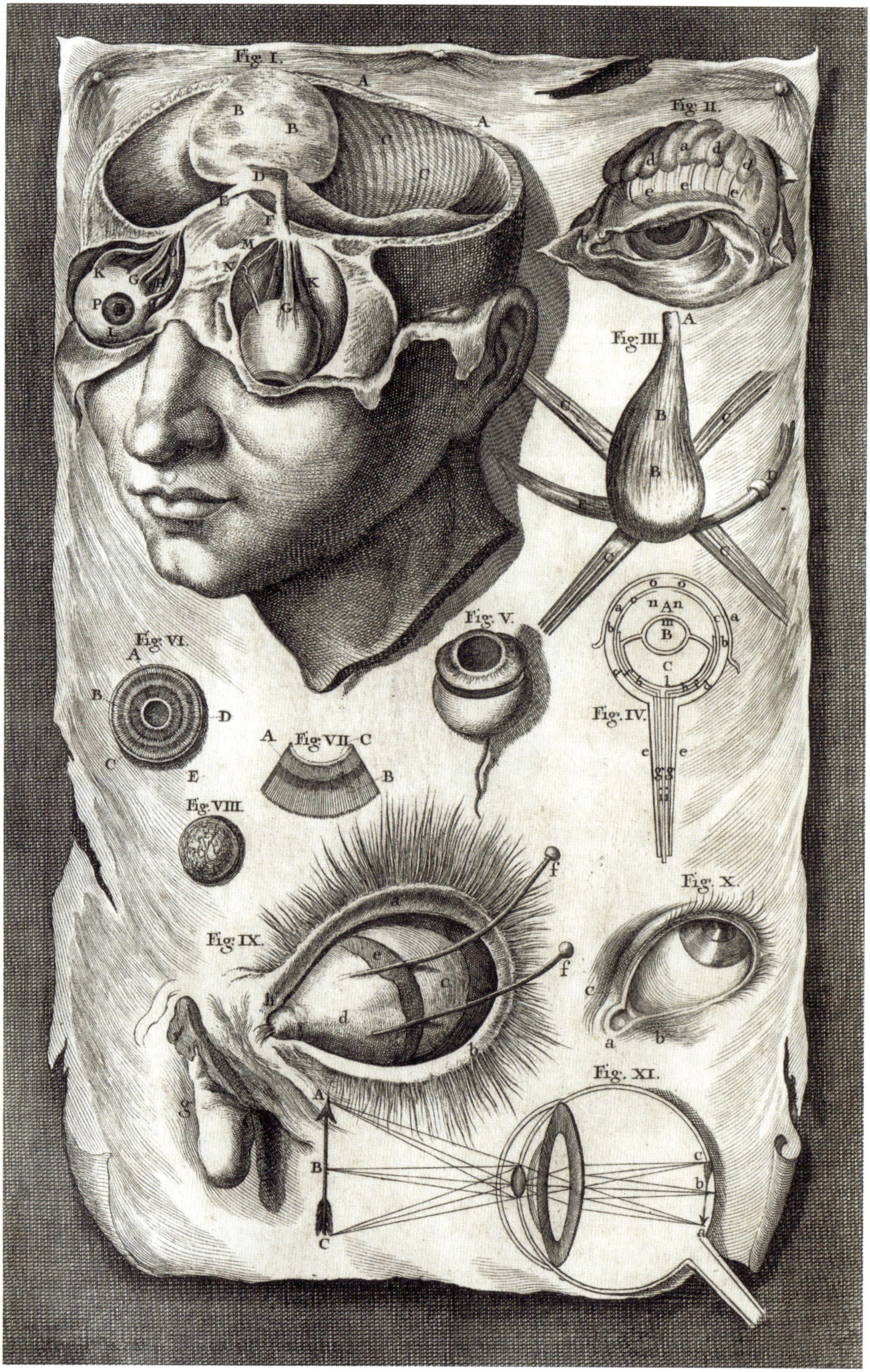

Physica Sacra (1731-1735) by Johann Jakob Scheuchzer is a fascinating blend of theology and natural history.

EXOTICA: 1, RELIGION: 0

Europe's Renaissance may be seen as a full-blown 'intellectual revolution' – one that was motivated by man, not the Church. Bit by bit, the Church as an institution lost its superiority to science. Faith and knowledge were no longer communicating vessels. As yet, no one had gone so far as to question the biblical account of the Creation. From a religious point of view the merest manifestation of *curiositas* – the very thing that drove the scholar and the collector – was to be deplored. Christianity castigated curiosity, regarding it as a vice. To the French philosopher and mathematician René Descartes (1596–1650), however, faith and scientific progress were not mutually exclusive: God simply existed beside the laws of nature, which science urgently ought to investigate, he thought.

A century later the Swiss physician and natural philosopher Johann Jakob Scheuchzer (1672–1733) was also wrestling with the tension between empiricism and faith. He combined his studies with elements from the Bible, which led to remarkable conclusions. Take his interpretation of fossils, for instance. Scheuchzer, who was renowned for his work as a palaeontologist, believed fossils to be leftovers from the Flood. His *Kupfer-Bibel* (or *Physica Sacra*, published between 1731 and 1735), was a commentary on the Bible based on the latest scientific insights of his day. He sought scientific explanations for the exotic animals, plants and miracles mentioned in the Bible – a rationale for Creation, for example, and for the serpent, the apple and the fig leaf in the famous scene between Adam and Eve. His book tried to show that the Bible was 'scientifically correct'. Not everyone was pleased by this, however; the Church labelled Scheuchzer a heretic.

—

NEW HORIZONS

The explorers of the late fifteenth century seem not to have been unduly worried about the 'sinfulness' of the curiosity that impelled them on their adventures, and they continued to set off into the unknown. Officially, their search for terra incognita was in order to spread Christianity; unofficially, it was a form of western imperialism. A key moment came in 1492 with Europe's discovery of America. The Italian explorer Christopher Columbus (1451–1506) had a hidden agenda for his mission: he was looking for a back door to trade between Asia and Europe, which traditionally went via the Silk Road. He risked his life to find a new westward passage to India – driven by the spirit of adventure, no doubt, but also by an underlying economic purpose. In 1492 that mission brought him not to Asia but to San Salvador in the Bahamas. Instead of Japan, Columbus reached Cuba. And although the Vikings had preceded him in the eleventh century, it was Columbus who paved the way for permanent contacts with the so-called New World. It was curiosity that made him broaden his own horizons – and those of the world then known.

C3
D2
D3
D4
H4
F1
F8
F2
F3
F4
G1
F5
F6
F7
H3
C5
D6
D7
F9
F10
H5
C6
C7
F11
G2
G3
E7
D10
H1
D9
D11
H7
B3
D8
D8
B4
D12
D13
H8
H14
H9
H13
H10
F12
F15
H12
C8
G4
G5
F13
F14
C9
D7
D14
D15
F18
F19
G6
F20
F21
F22
F17
H11
F16
F23
D18
16
D19
D18
D17
D20

SHELL SHOCK

Shells were very highly prized among collectors of exotica. They were not extremely expensive, but they were difficult to find. Ambroise Paré was captivated by them; in *Des monstres et prodiges* (1585) he wrote that 'There are to be found in the sea such strange and diverse kinds of shells that one can say that Nature, chambermaid of great God, plays in fabricating them.' Another influential book for shell collectors was written by the French scholar Antoine-Joseph Dézallier d'Argenville. In 1757 he wrote *La conchyliologie, ou Histoire naturelle des coquilles de mer, d'eau douce, terrestres et fossils.* In it he makes a rather odd distinction between collections of shells and collections of birds. It was perfectly fine to display birds 'artistically', perched on an artificial branch for instance, but shells should be arranged according to class and family, species by species. And the reason for this? Stuffed birds need looking after to save them from vermin, whereas shells neither rot nor decay.

<

In 1757, shells collectors could feast their eyes on the superb illustrations in Antoine-Joseph Dézallier d'Argenville's book of shells, *La conchyliologie.*

OLD WIVES' TALES

The medieval world was small: Europe and the Holy Land were the epicentres around which everything turned – even the sun. If there is one document that illustrates the way in which medieval man saw the Earth, it's the Hereford Mappa Mundi, drawn around 1285. This extraordinary world map gives us a detailed picture of the medieval worldview. It's the largest and most valuable medieval map still in existence – so valuable, in fact, that during the Second World War it was moved to a place of safety in a secret location.

The Mappa Mundi was not exactly a map by which to navigate; you couldn't fold it up and take it with you and it wouldn't prevent anyone from becoming hopelessly lost. But there are 420 cities and mythical places on it, such as the Garden of Eden and the Tower of Babel. Take a look at the edges too; there are countless bizarre drawings of exotic plants, hybrid animals and barbarian peoples. In India we see dragons, giants and dwarves; in Egypt a phoenix and a centaur; and in Africa hermaphrodites and amazons. In the Mediterranean a mermaid bobs around. The Turks are set down as 'descendants of Gog and Magog; a barbarous and unclean race devouring the flesh of youths and abortions'.

'At the farthest reaches of the world often occur new marvels and wonders,' wrote the English monk Ranulph Higden (1280–1364), 'as though nature plays with greater freedom secretly at the edges of the world than she does openly and nearer us in the middle of it.' This bears out what is on the Hereford Mappa Mundi. And it says a lot about what was generally believed then: the closer you came to the fringes of the world, the more exotic were the people, the animals and the plants you'd find there. More outlandish, more frightening, but also more attractive.

That's exactly how Gervase of Tilbury described the world in his *Otia Imperialia* or *Recreation for an Emperor* (1210), written to entertain Otto IV. The diverting book of marvels was an encyclopedia of the 'knowledge' of that time. A 'bagful of foolish old woman's tales' is what the German mathematician and philosopher Gottfried Wilhelm Leibniz (1646–1716) called it in 1700 or thereabouts – which only goes to show that it was still being read 490 years after it was written.

>

Google Earth anno 1285! The *Mappa Mundi* shows how medieval man saw the world: Jerusalem at the centre and a miscellany of marvellous creatures on the periphery.

Fabulous sea creatures, Nicolaes de Bruyn (1581-1656).

APPLE SMELLERS

Even now, in the twenty-first century, Gervase's wonderful list of 'exotica from all provinces' is a delight to read. We learn, for example, that the upper Ganges valley is the home of the gangines or 'apple smellers', whose only nourishment is the delicate fragrance of that fruit. And we make the acquaintance of the 'eale' or 'yale', which has one horn pointing forward and one backward. The yale 'comes from India, has a body like that of a horse, the jaws of a goat, the tail of an elephant and horns a cubit in length', Gervase informs us. Mythological beasts and monsters all seem to be denizens of distant climes, however; in Europe they're rather thin on the ground. The *Otia Imperialia* tells its marvelling readers all about phoenixes, dragons and suchlike improbable species. Of course, Gervase had not seen all these extraordinary creatures himself. His book was simply an amusing sampling of earlier sources, borrowing heavily from both the Bible and Germanic and Celtic sagas.

Gervase wrote the *Otia Imperialia* as pure entertainment, so Leibniz may have had a point in refusing to take it seriously. But the bottom line of the medieval book still applies to every collector of exotica (and reader of this book) today: man has an insatiable desire for the new, the rare and the strange. Amazement and entertainment still go hand in hand. How else do you explain the renewed popularity of taxidermy, for example?

—

RAW FOOD

If there's one thing we have in common with our medieval forebears, it's our penchant for monsters and the monstrous. One of the earliest treatises to catalogue and describe bizarre and exotic creatures was the eighth-century *Liber Monstrorum*. This immensely popular inventory of the outlandish and outré told of cyclops, satyrs, centaurs, cannibals and sciapods (men with one foot so large that they could lie on their back and use it as a sunshade), of ants born 'as big as dogs', sea creatures with the front end of a horse and the rear end of a fish, and 'strange' human races such as Ethiopians and pygmies. The author even claims to have known a hermaphrodite personally ... In all likelihood he had never set eyes on an Ethiopian or, indeed, on anyone whose physical characteristics differed much from his own. When it came to exotic peoples he gave his imagination free rein: 'There is a certain race of mixed nature on an island in the Red Sea', he tells us, 'who are said to be able to speak the languages of all nations. In this way they astonish people who come from afar, by naming their acquaintances, in order to deceive them, and eat them raw.'

EXOTIC FICTION

Few things were more appealing to medieval man than stories spiced with the exotic. They awoke his curiosity and supplied the stuff of his dreams – but they also aroused his fear of what was foreign or strange. The fact is that there was no way of checking the truth of such tales. First-hand information about distant places was rarer than hen's teeth. Virtually everything that was thought to exist on the fringes of the known world was derived from hearsay or from even less reliable sources. Indeed, some of those early travel accounts were blatant fictions. Certain authors made it a point of honour to exaggerate and embellish every detail. It was as if late-medieval writers were competing to see who could tell the tallest tales or produce the most mendacious superlatives. That explains the popularity of Gervase of Tilbury's *Otia Imperialia,* which was translated into the vernacular for those who couldn't read Latin. One such yarn-spinner was the Brabantine troubadour and poet Adenet le Roi (1240–1300), an author not given to false modesty: 'I have begun yet another book,' he announced, 'one that is very marvellous and diverse ... The tale is of great worth and most pleasing to hear. It is so varied and marvellous that I believe that no one has ever heard anything like it before.'

—

MANDEVILLE AND MARCO

Sir John Mandeville (1300–1371) belonged to the same club as Adenet. His *Book of Marvels and Travels* was one of the most popular works of the fourteenth century – and one of the most extreme examples of exotic fiction. It's a travelogue sexed up with a hefty dose of invention. Mandeville was perhaps the most accomplished embroiderer of narrative the world has ever seen. The *Travels* was copied, relished and extensively glossed. It may have been used as an introduction to geography, albeit a highly romanticized one. And to some who yearned for more than armchair adventure Mandeville's book was a clarion call. Not content with virtual exploration, they wanted the reality, to walk in Sir John's footsteps, brave his hazards. Like Christopher Columbus, for instance, who had read Mandeville's *Travels.*

It was the same story with the Venetian merchant Marco Polo (1254–1324). His four-volume *Livre des Merveilles du Monde,* familiar to English readers as *The Travels of Marco Polo,* epitomizes the art of exaggeration, possibly thanks to his co-author, the romance writer Rustichello of Pisa. Rulers, knights and clerics relished the heavily embellished stories of his journeys to Persia, China, Japan and India, made between 1276 and 1291. The traveller's tale with its chivalric overtones was enthusiastically read and copied out in monastic scriptoria. Columbus had this book in his collection too, and it may well have been the passages describing the extreme luxury to be found in the east that inspired him to search for a western route to Asia. As for the references to the cannibals and savage natives that would be encountered along the way, those are probably best passed over.

Morpho Menelaus. To wealthy patricians of the Renaissance and Baroque the name of that blue butterfly sounded as enticing as 'Porsche 911' does now.

GETTING STUFFED

In the nineteenth century stuffed animals and birds were all the rage. They filled not only the newly founded natural history museums and world fairs but collectors' homes too. In 1840 the naturalist William Swainson commented that 'In nothing has the growing taste for natural history so much manifested itself, as in the prevalent fashion of placing glass cases of beautiful birds and splendid insects on the mantelpiece or the side-table.' The craze for displaying stuffed animals in the home is alive and well in our own day and age too. Today, taxidermy is more popular than ever.

<

Still life with stuffed animals. Darwin, Sinke & van Tongeren, entitled: *Enraged Vari according to d'Hondecoeter.*

Hermaphrodites in *The Travels of Sir John Mandeville.*

BEYOND YOUR WILDEST DREAMS ...

Today we would be quick to label the xenophobic descriptions of barbarous races in travellers' tales as racist. But those stories may also be seen as a cocktail of exoticism and protectionism. Asia and Africa were both unknown and attractive in equal measure. 'The wonders of Africa and Asia are more various than those of Europe', wrote the German philosopher and theologian Albertus Magnus (1200–1280) in the thirteenth century. Medieval travels appealed to the imagination because they evoked fantasies about virgin territories with untold wealth and inexhaustible natural resources. But the fantasy did not end there. The thought of what might go on in the world's margins seems to have had a liberating effect on the imagination. Things could happen there that would be unthinkable – sinful, in other words – in Europe.

If you were to believe what you read, men copulated with beasts there and hermaphrodites hobnobbed with satyrs and other hybrid monstrosities. On the edges of the world the line between male and female, and human and animal, was indistinct and blurred. There were few restrictions or inhibitions, particularly sexual ones. And that exotic idea liberated the medieval reader's imagination.

WISH LIST

We shouldn't underrate the importance of texts such as these to the earliest collectors of exotica. They were their chief source of information. The 'facts' they contained determined many a wish list. Collectors had nothing else to go on, so they had little choice but to believe what they read. How else could they decide what they ought to have in their collections? For that matter, how could they even find out what existed, what there was to collect? There was no way of checking an object's origin, nor were there any first-hand accounts by the individuals who had acquired the exotic item from its source; objects came onto the market via seafarers, colonists and intermediaries. The more real contacts there were with the east in the late Middle Ages – not only armed conflicts and crusades, but trading contacts and voyages of discovery – the more opinion about those far-flung regions changed. Fear was replaced by fascination. A few intrepid souls set out, 'travel guide' in hand, to see for themselves those areas about which they had read so many enthralling stories. Was there really so much luxury and wealth there? Were there truly so many hermaphrodites? More to the point, how were those new areas to be defined? How did they fit into the European worldview?

—

PETRARCH

Wunderkammer. A splendid word – but what does it mean? Literally a room of wonders, intended to provoke curiosity and amazement and, of course, admiration for its owner's culture and learning. A collection depot where the passion for discovery, curiosity, exploration, exoticism and storytelling coalesce. A cabinet of rarities with which to flaunt one's erudition and cosmopolitan taste. In the late Middle Ages, rulers, nobles, churchmen and a handful of learned individuals began the systematic collection of marvellous objects and works of art of both human and natural origin to display in a *Wunderkammer* that was intended to summarize the world as it was known at that time. It was a sort of 'best of' the universe that enabled their owners (and their owners' visitors) to travel to exotic destinations, even if only in the mind – a 'curated selection' of all that the world had to offer in the fields of art, nature, scholarship and craftsmanship in all its hybrid forms.

Twelfth-century collectors were invariably princes or prelates such as the abbot of St Denis. In the fourteenth and especially the fifteenth century, collecting as an activity began to spread to other ranks of society as well. Most collectors belonged to the nobility or patriciate but the occasional intellectual also found the means to indulge his passion. Italian collectors tended to be scholars, apothecaries, physicians or men in the professions. This is how Lorenzo di Piero de' Medici came to know figures such as the writer Petrarch and the Venetian notary Oliviero Forzetta. Those physicists, natural philosophers and medical men were particularly keen on naturalia and exotica, which were more affordable than the gold and silver artificialia beloved of princely collectors.

O
P
O
P
S
S
S
S
O
P

*Curiosity is an inborn human trait
which is the daughter of ignorance
and the mother of knowledge.
Once wonder has opened our minds,
curiosity has this habit: observing an
extraordinary natural phenomenon –
such as a comet, a parhelion,
or a star at noon – our curiosity once asks
at once what it can mean or signify.*

Giambattista Vico, philosopher, 1668 – 1744

<

An attempt to explain the creation by means of natural theology in *Physica Sacra* (1731-1735).

UNIVERSAL THEATRE

John, Duke of Berry (1340–1416) belonged to the new generation of collectors. So great was his passion for art, antiquities and exotica, and so lavish his spending on them, that he was deeply in debt when he died. His collection included an ostrich egg, a snail shell, seven boars' tusks, porcupine spines, a massive tooth, a coconut, the jaw of a snake, red coral, a polar bear skin and three unicorn horns. Now this inventory reads like the sort of salmagundi of exotica that with a bit of luck you could pick up in a day. But then a collection such as that was a sign of social status, even perhaps of political, intellectual or religious prominence. A charismatic collection could *only* belong to a charismatic leader. A cleverly composed collection could *only* belong to a clever individual.

Rulers such as Francesco de' Medici, Albert V of Bavaria, Ferdinand II and the Emperor Rudolph II – all adroit manipulators of their images – each had a *Wunderkammer*, in Florence, Munich, Innsbruck and Prague respectively. Their cabinets overflowed with discoveries, large and small, expensive and inexpensive, uncommon and commonplace, living and dead. The inventories of those collections are more staggering than what remains of them now. They record a miscellany of stuffed animals, paintings, maps, clocks, scientific instruments and exotica; as well as precious objects in ivory, gold, ceramic, silver, coral, agate and mother-of-pearl. The purpose of the *Wunderkammer* was to create a miniature version of the world, with man as a leitmotif. A kind of ideal museum that the Flemish physicist Samuel von Quicchelberg strikingly referred to in 1565 as a 'universal theatre'. More than 450 years later, the show still goes on; collectors with a passion for the exotic are still among us.

—

NOT EXACTLY MODEST

The first modern Renaissance cabinets of curiosity were created in Italy in the late fifteenth and early sixteenth centuries by collectors such as Ulisse Aldrovandi, Francesco Calzolari and Ferrante Imperato. 'The eighth wonder of the world' is how Aldrovandi described his own *Wunderkammer*. He and Imperato were among the earliest sixteenth-century collectors to own a 'private museum'. 'Today in my microcosm, you can see more than 18,000 different things, among which 7000 plants in fifteen volumes, dried and pasted, 3000 of which I had painted as if alive', wrote Aldrovandi in 1595. A visitor put it as follows: 'His collection is a compendium of natural things, found above and beneath the earth, in the air and in the water.' Aldrovandi thought on a grand scale; he had informants who tipped him off about interesting objects. And he employed painters to document everything, among them his fellow-collector the apothecary Francesco Calzolari of Verona (1522–1609), who itemized his objects in what became the first published catalogue of a natural history collection. Calzolari's *museo* included not only many natural therapeutic and medicinal discoveries – herbs or plants that had a medicinal use – but also rare natural phenomena such as liquidambar, a lodestone (a naturally magnetized mineral) and a bezoar (a small stony concretion formed in a goat's stomach and used as an antidote for various ailments). When it came to his collection, modesty was not Francesco Calzolari's forte. The complimentary prolegomenon that preceded the catalogue proper, written by the Veronese physician Antonio Passieno, described it as: 'a most abundant repository and true treasury of all remarkable medicinal things, in which I observed each one placed in wonderful order in most decorative and elegant compartments and cases. Firstly, [Calzolari] sought exceptional herbs and then the rest from their own distant places and regions, sent to him as gifts from the greatest princes and rulers; here it is pleasing to see not a few whole plants and plant roots, rinds, hardened or liquid saps, gums, flowers, leaves, fruits and rare seeds and to recognize them as authentic. Also many metals. I omit how many dried terrestrial and aquatic animals I was astounded to find that I had never seen before.'

Portrait of Rudolf II by Giuseppe Arcimboldo, famous for his fruit and vegetable compositions.

METAL
METAL
LICA
COCHLEÆ
TURBINATA
ANIMALIUM PART
MUSEI
WORMIANI
HISTORIA
LUGD· BATAVORUM
EX OFFICINA ELSEVIRIA
Acad: Typog: 1655·

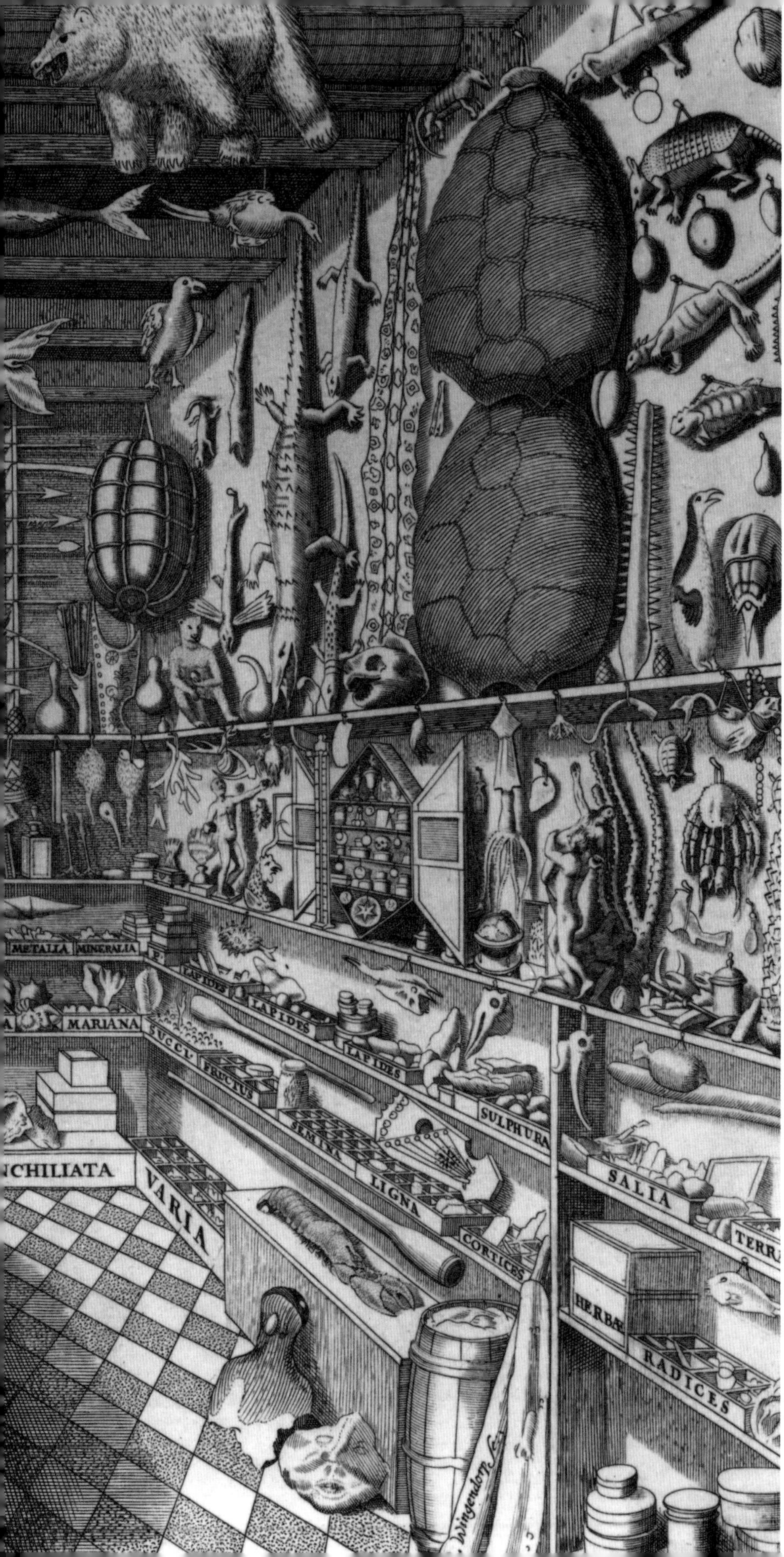

<
Ole Worm's (1588-1654) crowded private museum of naturalia and exotica.

BRIC-À-BRAC

'For in my opinion, the most ordinary things, the most common and familiar, if we could see them in their true light, would turn out to be the grandest miracles of nature and the most marvellous examples, especially as regards the subject of the action of men', declared the French philosopher and statesman Michel de Montaigne (1533–1592). He might as well have saved his breath: Renaissance collectors were avidly focused on the exotic. The ordinary or common or familiar rarely if ever featured in their collections. The usual kind of *Wunderkammer* can hardly be called representative, let alone encyclopedic or scientific. Very few collectors sought completeness in a particular area. The Italian mathematician-cum-astronomer-cum-philosopher Galileo Galilei (1564–1642) found that sort of amateurish collecting laughable; he derided those whose heterogeneous collections attested to nothing but their owners' pursuit of exoticism. 'They buy curiosities because they are rare or old. Or for some other reason, but the result is nothing more than bric-à-brac', he scoffed.

Call it bric-à-brac if you will; nonetheless, some collectors were very serious about their collections. And the fact is that most of them were fairly well organized – or were made to appear so to the outside world. Take Ole Worm (1588–1654), a Danish naturalist whose neatly ordered collection is immortalized in the posthumously published catalogue of his 'Museum Wormianum'. A double-page illustration shows a room crowded with rare and exotic things. The crocodile, turtle shells and armadillo displayed on the wall immediately catch the eye. But there are also clearly labelled boxes – for sea creatures and shells and minerals, for example. Everything in the collection was categorized and thematically arranged in drawers or on open shelves. After Worm's death his collection was bought by Frederick III of Schleswig-Holstein, who added it to his own equally tidy collection.

Ferdinand II of Austria (1529–1595) was also an ardent collector, who created a vast cabinet of curiosities in a purpose-built 'museum' in Schloss Ambras in Innsbruck. Here too every object was carefully categorized and arranged. To give just one example, the case of 'objects made of feathers' contained Aztec artefacts along with three stuffed birds of paradise. Ferdinand's *Wunderkammer* is still intact and in its original location in Schloss Ambras, and is one of the finest examples of a Renaissance collection.

'Wunderkammer', a drawing by the Argentinian contemporary artist Santiago Caruso.

SANGUINARY SEAWEED

It must be said that the way objects were ordered was still artificial. This was a topic much discussed among collectors. Obviously everyone – even the non-naturalist – could tell a rock from a bird or a piece of scientific apparatus from a skilfully crafted work of art. But the wonder was in the objects that somehow defied categorization, things that could not immediately be defined as animal, vegetable or mineral. Coral, for instance: is that a plant or an animal? Or is it, as the Roman poet Ovid believed, petrified seaweed, turned to red stone by the blood that dripped from Medusa's severed head? And is a gilded coconut a work of nature's art or of the goldsmith's?

Craftsmen pitted their skills against nature by 'ennobling' naturalia such as coconuts. They treated exotica in all manner of ingenious and artful ways – polishing, chasing, carving, engraving ... A nautilus shell might be mounted on a silver foot, a rhinoceros horn turned into a lidded goblet. Rhino horns were carved into medallions or drinking cups. Elephant tusks became exquisite ivory works of art, if possible even more beautiful than God's creation. What it all came down to was that man – God's highest creation – could do better than nature. Or at least hold his own with it. In fact, he could even effect an upgrade: shells that came from regions inhabited by 'savages' could be 'improved'. Man competed with an exotic world of which he had little or no real knowledge. His underlying purpose? To emphasize his own pre-eminence.

—

THE CURIOSITY CABINET

If there was neither the space nor the money for a real *Wunderkammer*, the aspiring collector could always fall back on option 2: a cabinet. A purpose-built cupboard was also a place in which to house and display a collection, though in the shape of a compact piece of furniture rather than an entire room. These literal 'curiosity cabinets' were often exquisitely made, both inside and out. The cabinet presented to King Gustavus Adolphus of Sweden (1594–1632) a few months before his death became an instant legend. Perhaps the most spectacular art cabinet ever built, it was hailed at the time as the eighth wonder of the world, though admittedly that epithet was applied to many marvellous objects. Wonder or not, it combined the finest workmanship then available. For six years master craftsmen laboured to assemble the 240 cm high and 120 cm wide cabinet under the direction of merchant, diplomat and collector Philipp Hainhofer of Augsburg (1578–1647). Hainhofer was not himself a gifted goldsmith or joiner. His metier was production management. He knew where to find the best craftsmen for the job – the thirty or so goldsmiths and silversmiths, cabinet-makers, glass-blowers, lapidaries, miniaturists, enamellers, contrivers of clockwork and automata whose skills were brought to the task – and which specialist international dealers to go to for the prestigious exotica that were to ornament the cabinet. He found shells in Frankfurt, bought coral in Marseille. The cabinet's exterior was lavishly inlaid with medallions of Limoges enamel and intarsia panels of exotic woods, along with agate, marble, lapis lazuli, rock crystal and gold. And, crowning it all, a 'naturalia summit' of corals, minerals and seashells supported a silver-mounted Seychelles nut transformed into a vessel for Venus. Thus the outside of the cabinet immediately proclaimed that here was an immensely precious luxury object. The interior was also decorated, though less flamboyantly, for this is where the cabinet's true wonder lay – in the countless drawers and compartments with their false bottoms and secret recesses, behind the sliding panels and reversible doors, and the doors and drawers beyond them. These contained exquisite and often specially made artificialia and naturalia, including a nautilus-shell cup and a mummified monkey's claw. In 1695 the Augsburg cabinet – one of the most extravagant masterpieces of its time – entered the collection of Uppsala university in Sweden, where it may still be seen today.

Shell cabinet, *circa* 1690.

FOLLOWERS OF FASHION

There were trends in exotica collecting, as in every other kind of collection. At first, the vogue for exotica was more or less dictated by whatever was brought back by the ships that returned from voyages of discovery, when novel exotic collectibles were constantly to be had. In the sixteenth century a unicorn's horn – a narwhal tusk – was every collector's holy grail. Again thanks to journeys of exploration, in the seventeenth century a good deal of oriental exotica came onto the market. In the nineteenth century seaweeds, anemones, mosses and ferns were all the botanical rage. Taxidermy of both exotic and indigenous animals became immensely popular in the mid-nineteenth century. In the early twentieth century the craze was for tribal art from Africa, Oceania and the polar regions.

<

Choix de coquillages by Alexandre Isidore Leroy de Barde (1777-1828), watercolour and gouache on paper, from the collection of the Louvre.

NATURE: ARTIST OR ARTWORK?

The classic *Wunderkammer* – which is to say the collections of the sixteenth and seventeenth centuries – contained a vast miscellany of objects. Exotica, of course, but also antiquities and examples of exceptional workmanship – things produced by both nature and art, and preferably a combination of both. In 1599 the Neapolitan collector Ferrante Imperato (1525–1615) found that 'art conduces to the perfection of stones and metals'. Nature could be embellished with gold, silver and exotic wood. An artist could turn a magnificent piece of ivory – a collector's item in itself – into a bravura display of bas-relief carving. Anyone who could command the requisite craftsmanship could put his stamp on nature. In other words, nature could be surpassed by art. Nature was makeable and malleable. Man simply stole away with the finest that nature displayed, determined to have the final say, even if only by making a base or box for a rare shell or stone. What was a work of art made by nature? And what was a work of art made by man? Was nature an artist or an artwork? This was the sort of question a collector would pose to those who entered his chamber of wonders.

Botanists also discovered that nature could be man-made. Not only did they record and collect existing plant and tree varieties, they also began to experiment with cross-breeding different species. They played God with their plants, sometimes with startling knock-on effects, such as the tulip mania that swept the Dutch Republic in the seventeenth century; speculators traded the rare bulbs for extraordinary sums of money until the market suddenly collapsed – the first example of an economic bubble.

—

GIANTS AND DWARVES

Exotica belonged to the realm of the *Wunderkammer*. But in fact, the idea goes a lot further, for it reflects the way we interact with strange cultures and use collectors' items to define our own. We associate the exotic with discovery and curiosity, but also with luxury from parts unknown – and, indirectly, with colonialism and geopolitics.

René I of Anjou (1409–1480), duke, artist and notorious lover of all things exotic, was an exemplary collector in that respect. We need only look at his court: the princely household included dwarves, giants, child prodigies, a 'pinhead' and Moorish slaves. The fauna category was also very well represented, with lions, leopards, monkeys, ostriches, civet cats and wild African goats.

>

Colourful exotic birds from the book by Dutch apothecary and collector Albertus Seba (1665-1736).

TAB. LXVII.
Fig. 1.
Fig. 2.
Fig. 3.
Fig. 4.

Tulips and shells were highly-prized, exotic luxury goods.
Right: A parasol-like amaryllis, recorded by Robert Jacob Gordon in South Africa.

Cyrtanthus

PHILIP THE GOOD, THE DECADENT DUKE

The court of Philip the Good, duke of Burgundy (1396–1467), was also renowned for the number of exotic characters that could be found in it at any given moment. In addition to his troupe of 'Saracen' *morisque* dancers he had at least twenty-four dwarves and fools. They included Madame d'Or, the blonde dwarf who belonged to Philip's third wife, Isabella of Portugal, and his own giant, named Hans. Philip turned his passion for exotica (and giants and dwarves) to diplomatic and political ends, impressing foreign visitors to his court with his precious collection. An account by the chroniclers of an emissary of the king of Bohemia to the Brussels court is eye-opening: 'a side table had been set up overflowing with countless costly vessels and other things impossible to describe. ... When [the emissary of the king of Bohemia] had eaten ... [the duke] dispatched him to see his zoological garden, which is of vast proportions with many fountains and lakes, in which one found all manner of birds and animals which seemed strange to us. Afterwards, the duke caused his treasure and jewels to be shown, which are beyond measure, so much so that one might say that he far outdid the Venetian's treasure in precious stones and pearls. It is said that nowhere else in the world were such costly treasures ... which were so abundant that we never thought to see the like.'

More decadent still was the wedding banquet prepared for the nuptials of Duke Philip and Isabella of Portugal in Bruges on 7 January 1430. It was an object lesson in showing off. The climax came with the entrance of an enormous pie that opened to reveal a live sheep, its fleece dyed blue and its horns gilded, followed by a mock battle between Hans, the duke's giant, and Madame d'Or, Isabella's dwarf – a symbolic spectacle to celebrate the joining of the Burgundian and Portuguese houses. All of this was as nothing compared to the truly awesome extravagance of Philip's 'Feast of the Pheasant', held in February 1454 as a kind of promotional event for his planned crusade against the Ottoman empire, which had captured Constantinople the previous year. Eastern and western themes were interwoven in a far from subtle manner. The banquet was to be the last word in luxury, a feast that defied imagination. There are numerous anecdotes describing the live acts that featured real camels and a real elephant and other exotic creatures.

—

MARINERS AS EXOTICA MERCHANTS

One of the best-known collectors of exotica and naturalia is undoubtedly Albertus Seba (1665–1736). Seba was an apothecary from Friesland who prepared his remedies and restoratives with natural ingredients. He learned his craft from fellow apothecaries in Nuremberg, Strasbourg and Groningen before settling in Amsterdam. As the raw materials he needed for his preparations came from all over the globe, he began to collect rarities from nature. Soon, his collection far exceeded what was needed to brew medicines. His pharmacy in Amsterdam, opened in 1697, was so famous that he even had Peter the Great, the tsar of Russia (1672–1725), as a customer. Seba devised a canny way of acquiring exotic raw materials and objects. He took no money for treating the complaints and diseases of mariners who sailed into the port of Amsterdam, accepting instead the exotica they brought back from their distant destinations. The seventeenth century was a golden age for Amsterdam. The Dutch East India Company, founded in 1602, was an important catalyst in this development. It also enabled Seba to acquire exotica from every corner of the world, from Indonesia to South America, from the Caribbean to Central America, from North America to Sri Lanka, and from North and West Africa. The new Dutch colonies, such as Essequibo (1625), Curaçao (1634), Ceylon (1658) and Suriname (1667), were veritable gold-mines for exotica. Via their trading posts, an abundance of herbs, textiles, exotic products and knowledge from the overseas territories entered the northern Netherlands. All to the good for commerce, art and science.

—

COLLECTION BOOK WITH FAKES

It's worth taking a look at the history of the apothecary-collector's cabinet of curiosities. In the early 1730s, after decades of collecting, Seba commissioned illustrations of every specimen and arranged for the publication of a four-volume catalogue. It was the most complete book of its kind, one of the eighteenth century's greatest natural history achievements. 'My collection includes all manner of exquisite items from the East and West Indies,' he wrote, 'among them no fewer than seven hundred jars containing the rarest exotic animals and many particularly rare snakes. Also exceptionally rare shells. And the finest and most complete collection of butterflies from the four corners of the world.' There were even fabulous beasts, such as a hydra and a dragon.

In fact, the catalogue described Seba's second collection. In 1717 he had sold his first to a particularly illustrious customer, Peter the Great. With the proceeds he immediately began building a second, even bigger collection, consisting mainly of exotic sea creatures, reptiles and insects. Great achievement though it indubitably is, however, the 'inventory' needs to be taken with a pinch of salt, for not everything it describes was in Seba's own collection. Some illustrations were simply copied from other sources, such as the picture of the seven-headed hydra brazenly 'borrowed' from the catalogue of a Hamburg collector. Moreover, very few of the other creatures had been drawn from life, the artists having made do with preserved specimens – hence the mistakes in morphology or colour, as you can see in the illustrations of some of the snakes. For instance, the reptiles had lost their original colour as a result of being pickled in alcohol.

A seven-headed hydra, one of the remarkable fake creatures drawn 'from life' in Albertus Seba's (1665-1736) collection book.

Nature wishes that one should
admire such things,
but not that one should understand them

Boetius de Boodt (1550–1632) of Bruges, mineralogist,
on his fascination with crystals

<

The goldsmith Joachim Hiller's magnificent nautilus cup
in the form of an ostrich, *circa* 1600.

N.° 4.
N.° 7.
N.° 8
N.° 9.

<

Studies of a puffer fish from the catalogue of the collection of Albertus Seba (1665-1736).

>

Wunderkammer, work by contemporary Belgian artist Tom Liekens.

Chapter 2

WONDERS OF THE AMERICAS

Exotica from North to South

If the other islands we have seen are very beautiful and green and fertile, then this is much more so, with great groves of trees, very green. There are some large lakes here and around and overlooking them there are marvellous woods. Here and in all the island everything is green and the vegetation is like April in Andalusia. And the singing of the birds is such that it would seem that a man would never wish to leave here. And the flocks of parrots that darken the sun, and birds of so many kinds so different from our own that it is a marvel! And then there are trees of a thousand kinds all producing their own kind of fruit, and all wonderfully aromatic; I am the saddest man in the world at not recognizing them, because I am certain that they are all of value, and I am bringing samples of them, and of the herbs.

Christopher Columbus, 21 October 1492

<

The expedition to Brazil and Peru of explorer and botanist Carl Friedrich Philipp von Martius (1794–1868), as pictured in his standard work *Historia Naturalis Palmarum*.

In 1492 Christopher Columbus (1451–1506) dropped anchor off the eastern seaboard of Asia, or so he believed. That he was mistaken is something he never knew, for at the time no one could have told him any different. If we peep over his shoulder as he pens his log, a few things instantly become clear: firstly, he is obviously impressed by what he sees; secondly, he has the wrong end of the geographical stick; and, thirdly, in some respects the descriptions in his logbook appear remarkably similar to those of Marco Polo (1254–1324), written two centuries earlier – with the same style, the same amazement and the same degree of hyperbole.

Columbus did bring specimens of exotic plants and animals back to Europe. Needless to say, they were of intense interest to scholars, students and collectors – men such as Ulisse Aldrovandi (1522–1605), professor of natural history at Bologna's university and an avid collector, who pointed out that there was 'a great field for the scholars of this and future centuries, since Christopher Columbus and others, with the greatest effort, expense and danger, have discovered as it were another world, in which such remarkable wonders have been disclosed and discovered and described and brought back to us'.

The discovery of America (not East Asia, as Columbus had mistakenly believed) caused tremendous excitement in Europe, and not only among scholars such as Aldrovandi. Suddenly, the Earth had become a whole lot bigger. As for its shape, Columbus had arrived at a startling conclusion. 'It is not round,' he wrote, 'but of the form of a pear ... upon part of which is a prominence like a woman's nipple.'

—

FALLOW GROUND

Columbus's voyage to the new continent gave him the reputation of a scholarly pioneer, which was far from being his aim. His intention had been to sail westward until he reached the Indies, in hopes of finding a maritime shortcut for the traffic along the Silk Road. His discovery of the new lands certainly led to commercial exploitation.

The discovery of the New World more or less coincided with the advent of printing. Each of those things enhanced the other. Books and expeditions not only caused collectors to seek artefacts and naturalia from hitherto unknown parts; they also inspired artists, who gave their imagination free rein in representing the new lands and their inhabitants.

>

Illustration from Ulisse Aldrovandi's *Monstrorum Historia* (1642).

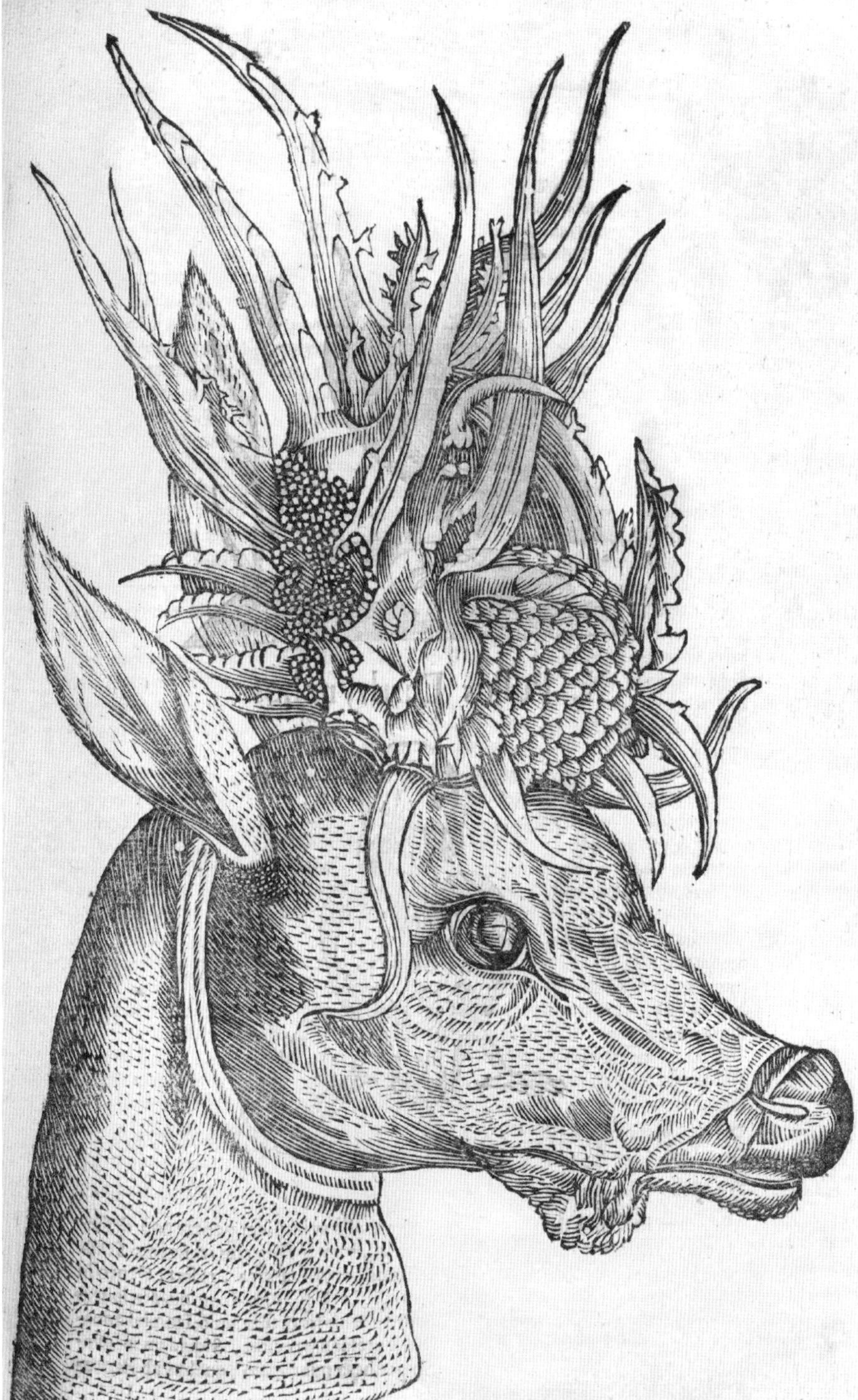

'America Riding on an Armadillo', a drawing by Adrian Collaert (1560-1618).

ARMADILLO WANTED

The exploration of the New World introduced collectors to a whole host of new must-haves. Early enthusiasts were quick to snap up exotic souvenirs from newly discovered lands. To their selection of rhinoceros and unicorn horns from Asia, they added creatures such as the armadillo – like the alligator, one of the most typical examples of American naturalia.

In the print collection of New York's Metropolitan Museum of Art is a somewhat fanciful engraving of a scantily clad huntress riding a giant armadillo. Dating from around 1584, it's by Adriaen Collaert (1560–1618) of Antwerp, after a design by Maerten de Vos (1532–1603). Such allegorical renderings of the 'Four Continents' were highly popular in the sixteenth century and later. They illustrate the ways in which we have perceived exotic regions through the centuries. Conspicuous in this print are the feathered headdress and the parrot, along with the weapons and the grisly use to which they're put. The engraving of Africa from the same 'Four Continents' series shows another barely covered female figure mounted on a crocodile, with chameleons, griffins and troglodytes in the background.

(NO) SMOKING

Tobacco also arrived as an exotic curiosity from America. Colonists traded with the native Americans for it, making a tidy profit in the process. It was not without reason that the Indians' tobacco was called 'brown gold'. Bartolomé de las Casas (1484–1566), a historian and Dominican missionary who exposed the oppression by Europeans of the native peoples in the Americas, described what he witnessed in Cuba around 1510: 'they suck, absorb or receive that smoke inside with the breath, by which they become benumbed and almost drunk, and so it is said they do not feel fatigue', he wrote. 'These, muskets as we will call them, they call *tabacos*.'

It was not long before the addictive habit spread to the rest of the world. Tobacco reached Spain around 1528, Japan in 1542 and Paris in 1559. Walter Ralegh (1554–1618) introduced tobacco to England in 1578, though not everyone was a fan of the so-called 'medicinal herb'. King James I and VI inveighed against its use in his famous anti-tobacco polemic entitled *A Counterblaste to Tobacco*, published in 1604, in which he denounced the 'filthy novelty' of smoking as 'A custom loathsome to the eye, hateful to the nose, harmful to the brain, dangerous to the lungs, and in the black stinking fume thereof, nearest resembling the horrible Stygian smoke of the pit that is bottomless.'

—

COME FOR DINNER ...

'When [the dead captive] has been skinned, a man takes him and cuts off the legs above the knees, and the arms at the body. Then ... they part the back, including the buttocks, from the front part and divide this [rear part] amongst themselves. However, the women keep the innards, simmer them, and make a type of broth.'

That the German soldier and sailor Hans Staden (1525–1576) made it back home to tell his fearful tale is a wonder in itself. In 1552 the Portuguese ship on which he was serving as a gunner was wrecked off the Brazilian island of São Vicente. Not long afterwards, while on a hunting expedition, he was caught by the Tupinambá, who customarily feasted on their victims' flesh. In his account of his captivity, Staden tells of being served with some delicious soup. Only as he swallowed the last drops did he discover bits of a shipmate's skull at the bottom of his bowl. The Tupinambá had brewed up a batch of man-broth. Staden's fate seemed sealed, but he managed to escape in the nick of time and was rescued by a French ship.

The tale of his adventures was published in 1557 under the sensational title of *Warhaftige Historia und beschreibung eyner Landtschafft der Wilden Nacketen, Grimmigen Menschfresser-Leuthen in der Newenwelt America* (*True Story and Description of a Country of Wild, Naked, Grim, Man-eating People in the New World, America*). An instant best-seller, it was translated into several languages and ran to no fewer than seventy-six editions. Tasty stuff!

In 1636 the artist Frans Post went to Brazil. He travelled throughout the new Dutch colony, painting its animals, landscapes and plants.

INDIGENOUS BRAZILIANS, ENGLISH DOLLS

More often than not, expeditions to new lands would include artists whose task was to make a visual record of the landscapes, peoples, plants, animals and natural phenomena they encountered. They were often pressed for time and had to work hard to get everything down on paper. Some of them produced a very special oeuvre that continues to appeal to exotica enthusiasts. Take John White (1540–1593), for instance. That English colonial and cartographer is perhaps best known for his detailed drawings of the American coastline. The real extent of his abilities was demonstrated in a series of splendid watercolours of indigenous Americans, which is now in the British Museum in London. His paintings provide unique evidence of how sixteenth-century North-American peoples lived. Yet there is something strange about his pictures. Were they to impress Queen Elizabeth back home? Were they meant to encourage English colonists? Or do they augur the fate that would later befall North America's indigenous population?

—

PRIMITIVE CANNIBALS

When Jean de Léry, a French Protestant pastor and writer, went to Brazil in 1578, he was determined to find new minerals and plants in the recently founded French colony of France Antarctique, near Rio de Janeiro. Not only did he discover a good many plants and animals, but also anthropophagous tribes who had never seen European settlers before. Secretly, De Léry was also on the lookout for new medicinal ingredients, because he knew that European apothecaries would be more than happy to use them in their preparations. He was quietly hoping to find as much in the way of extraordinary medicines in America as came from Asia, which provided such panaceas as powdered rhino horn and bezoars (a small stone formed in a goat's stomach). As De Léry's mission subtly shows, Brazil was perceived very differently from Asia. Books and travel accounts, even the early curiosity cabinets, all portrayed the new land in a far from flattering light. The indigenous Brazilians were depicted as jungle-dwelling savages or primitive cannibals – to say nothing of the poisonous plants and dangerous beasts that infested the country. Fascinating, but also frightening, this was the perfect cocktail for exotica collectors and adventurers such as De Léry.

Asia's image in the Renaissance could hardly be more different. China, Japan and South-East Asia were depicted as rich regions on a cultural par with Europe. We can see that in still-life paintings in which costly *aziatica* appear – pepper, shells, lacquerware, porcelain, and utensils used in tea ceremonies.

HISTORIA NATVRALIS
BRASILIAE,
Auſpicio et Beneficio
ILLVSTRISS. I. MAVRITII COM. NASSAV
ILLIVS PROVINCIÆ ET MARIS SVMMI PRÆFECTI ADORNATA.
In qua
Non tantum Plantæ et Animalia, ſed et In-
digenarum morbi, ingenia et mores deſcribuntur et
Iconibus ſupra quingentas illuſtrantur.
LVGDVN. BATAVORVM,
Apud Franciſcum Hackium
et
AMSTELODAMI,
Apud Lud. Elzevirium. 1648.

POST FROM BRAZIL

In the absence of yet-to-be-invented photography and video, colonial expeditions would very often take artists along. They produced prints and drawings that are still sought after by exotica collectors today. The Haarlem-born artist Frans Post (1612–1680) is a good example. He went to Brazil as part of the entourage of the new Dutch governor, John Maurice of Nassau-Siegen (1604–1679), who administered the colony from 1636 to 1644. The Dutch republic had just captured Portuguese-held territory in Brazil and established a colony for the Dutch West India Company, founded in 1621. John Maurice came to inspect the situation and bring stability, but mainly to see how he could extend Dutch territory. He sent out a series of expeditions from the capital, which he renamed Mauritsstad – Maurice Town. Brazilian sugar plantations were particularly profitable, so he built the infrastructure that was needed to exploit the natural resources to the full. That also required slaves, who were brought from Angola.

Frans Post made a visual record of the entire expedition. His lush Brazilian landscapes are probably his best-known works. But when the holdings of the Noord-Hollands Archief in Haarlem were digitized, thirty-four entirely unknown drawings by Post were discovered, accompanied by the artist's own comments. They show just how amazed he was by the local flora and, especially, the fauna. Post's drawings of a macaque ('very friendly and pleasant'), a porcupine, an armadillo ('tastes like chicken'), a capybara, and a jaguar ('very cruel, destructive and strong') still look very fresh.

—

REFERENCE WORK

Besides Frans Post and John Maurice of Nassau-Siegen, there were other well-known people aboard the Brazil-bound ship – namely the Dutch physician and botanist Willem Piso (1611–1678) and the German geographer Georg Marggraf (1610–1644). Together they took part in the very first zoological and botanical expedition to Brazil, which led to the publication in 1648, after Marggraf's death, of the *Historia naturalis Brasiliae*, a book that would remain the standard work of reference on Brazil until the nineteenth century. It featured poisonous plants, dangerous snakes, bloodthirsty cannibals and Dutch sugar-cane plantations; in the decades following its publication its illustrations inspired numerous artists to produce 'exotic' works of art.

<

Cannibals, poisonous plants and sugarcane: the *Historia Naturalis Brasiliae* (1648) makes for exciting reading about Brazil – at that time still untouched.

DIPLOMATIC COCONUT

This is a very special coconut. For one thing, in the seventeenth century a coconut was a costly item, worthy to be mounted in precious metal. For another, the relief carving depicts indigenous Brazilians. Some display cannibalistic traits while others are more 'civilized', wearing clothes and eating wholesome food. If you look closely you can even pick out a European woman handing a fish to a Brazilian – as if the Brazilians couldn't fish for themselves. The coconut was meant to show how the Dutch were spreading civilization in Brazil. The man who commissioned this masterpiece was John Maurice of Nassau-Siegen. He intended it as a diplomatic gift that would highlight his status as governor of the Dutch colony in Brazil in the eyes of other rulers. The man who designed the scenes depicted on it was the Dutch artist Albert Eeckhout (1610–1665), who was also part of John Maurice's 1636–1644 mission. Like Frans Post, he was there to provide a visual account of the peoples, landscape and animals in the new Dutch colony.

—

ENIGMATIC EASTER ISLAND

Easter Sunday 1722. The Dutch explorer Jacob Roggeveen (1659–1729) accidentally landed on a Polynesian island off the coast of Chile. Appropriately enough, he named it Easter Island. In the centuries since, that name alone has fostered the mystery that surrounds the island, which has been visited by many explorers but never really understood. James Cook stopped off there in 1774 and reported that for some inexplicable reason the famous statues had been toppled over. One of his crew even managed to communicate with the island's indigenous inhabitants, the Rapa Nui. The artist William Hodges (1744–1797), who was sailing with Cook, painted the earliest-known picture of Easter Island. On a later voyage, John Linton Palmer (1824–1903), a ship's doctor with the British Navy, found the islanders 'friendly, engaging and happy', though he did discover traces of cannibalism.

>

Coconuts were rare and costly items. Sometimes they were beautifully carved and mounted in gold or silver, becoming exquisite works of art.

N° 2
N° 3
N° 4
N° 5
N° 6
N° 7
N° 8
9
N° 10
N° 11
N° 12
13
♀
N° 14
N° 15
N° 16
17
N° 18
♀
N° 19
N° 20
21
N° 22
N° 23
N° 24

GENIUS

If anyone in the eighteenth century exemplified the exotica spirit, it was Alexander von Humboldt (1769–1859). The Prussian explorer and naturalist was adept in geography, as well as physics, geology and biology. Not for nothing did Charles Darwin call him 'the greatest scientific traveller who ever lived'. His scientific expeditions to South and Central America were famous, and he published extensively about them. On the Orinoco river and in the impenetrable jungle, Humboldt and his party often risked their lives in the name of science. 'In Guyana', he wrote, 'the mosquitoes abound in such clouds as to darken the air ... the attacks of these insects render it impossible to hold the pen steadily.' It was little short of a miracle that Humboldt survived. He suffered altitude sickness as he crossed the Andes, caught electric eels and sometimes had nothing but rice and bananas to live on. His passion for adventure led to thrilling stories and sensational discoveries, including the ruins of Inca settlements. Nevertheless, his magnum opus was the multi-volume *Kosmos*, a work of genius in which he sought to combine diverse branches of knowledge into a single universal vision of the world.

<

Insects illustrated in *The Naturalist on the River Amazons* (1863), a groundbreaking study of the Amazon basin by Henry Walter Bates (1825-1892).

FEATHERED HARMONY?

This flamboyantly feathered gathering probably illustrates one of Aesop's fables, but it could just as easily be an exotic interpretation of the familiar saying by the Dutch poet Jacob Cats (1577–1660) that *Elck vogeltge singt soo 't gebeckt is* – which loosely translated means every bird sings with the beak it's been given. The painting, called *The Concert of Birds,* is by Jan van Kessel I and is now in the Royal Museum of Fine Art in Antwerp. It's a bit different from traditional seventeenth-century animal paintings by the likes of Frans Snijders and Jan Fyt. The conductor of this concert party is the owl clutching the open score. Perched all around him is a company of native and exotic birds – a toucan, a scarlet macaw, a swan, an Amazon parrot, a peacock, magpies and many many more – all twittering and tweeting and warbling and screeching. Altogether a fine bunch of feathered artistes, arranged just as their stuffed counterparts might have been in a *Wunderkammer*. You'd have to be an expert to realize that the birds in the painting are not exactly renowned for the sweetness of their song. There's the irony: while it looks as if they're all singing in harmony from the same score, they're really producing an ear-splitting cacophony. So what we have here is a work about our inability to communicate.

While we're on the topic of difficult avian scores ... Athanasius Kircher (1601/2–1680) attempted to write down the birdsong he heard in the form of musical notation. In his influential musicological book entitled *Musurgia Universalis* (1650) he transformed the call of the nightingale, chicken, quail, macaw and cuckoo into 'music'. The rooster received 15 notes, the nightingale at least 260, over six staves.

>

An owl conducts a choir of birds that are not renowned for their sweet singing: symbolism at its most pointed in this *The Concert of Birds* by Jan van Kessel I.

JAMES INTO THE WILD

'However rude it is, America will always be my land. I never close my eyes without travelling thousands of miles along our noble streams and traversing our noble forests.' Patriotic words, especially for an adventurer who grew up in France. With *The Birds of America*, John James Audubon (1785–1851) produced a sort of prequel to *Walden: Life in the Woods* by Henry David Thoreau, published in 1854. Audubon's ambitious idea was to catalogue all the birds of America in a single book – an absurdly optimistic plan, especially given how difficult travelling in America was at that time. Yet he persevered, and the result is immensely impressive: *The Birds of America* contains 435 life-sized, hand-coloured plates. Audubon endured appalling hardships in order to show the hitherto unknown birds in their natural habitat. Today, largely as a result of that extraordinary endeavour, he is still regarded as America's greatest naturalist. It's Audubon we have to thank for this unique watercolour of the Carolina parrot, for example. It dates from 1811. Less than a century later – in 1904 – this bird was extinct.

James Audubon was raised in France. Much of his childhood was spent roaming the countryside for hours on end. In the Napoleonic period he fled France to avoid conscription, travelling on a false passport obtained by his father. He went to Philadelphia, where his family had a farm. James was not much help on the farmstead; instead he spent all his time in the woods looking for natural specimens, rifle in one hand, painting kit in the other. It's particularly noteworthy that in the nineteenth century Audubon was already considering the consequences of the industrial revolution; he saw America gradually becoming urbanized and overhunted. Finally the Carolina parrot died out.

\>

The Carolina Parrot, drawn by James Audubon (1785-1851), became extinct in the wild in 1904. The last captive specimen died in 1918.

ASTONISHING AMAZON

Columbus had obviously read Marco Polo's travels. But what inspired the young English naturalists and explorers Henry Walter Bates (1825–1892) and Alfred Russel Wallace (1823–1913) to cross the Atlantic? Both men had been fired with enthusiasm by *A Voyage up the River Amazon*, the account of a journey up that great river by William Henry Edwards, published in 1847. Bates and Wallace aimed to make their own, equally thorough exploration of the Amazon rainforest. They made meticulous preparations. They sold preserved specimens to help pay for the trip. They visited all the European collections of South American plants and animals they could. And they compiled wish lists of birds and animals to bring back for collectors and museums. At last they were ready to leave, sailing from Liverpool in the spring of 1848, bound for the Amazon. Once arrived, they spent some time collecting together before splitting up to explore separately.

Wallace returned to England in 1852, but after almost a month at sea fire broke out in the hold and the order was given to abandon ship. All Wallace could do was watch helplessly from a small open boat as his precious insects and plants and journals went up in smoke: 'everything was gone', he wrote sadly, 'and I had not one specimen to illustrate the unknown lands I had trod, or to call back the recollection of the wild scenes I had beheld!'

Bates's journals fared better and survived the journey home. They are full of drawings of the exotic fauna of the Amazon basin, and became the basis for *The Naturalist on the River Amazons*, which according to Darwin was one of the most ground-breaking studies ever carried out in that region. In total, Bates described well over fourteen thousand species, of which more than half were new to science. Even today, enthusiasts whose taste runs to South American exotica find food for thought in his observations.

<

The naturalist and explorer Henry Walter Bates (1825-1892) in action with toucans.

The island of Gili Asahan in Indonesia, by photographer Tommaso Riva.

MARVELS OF THE DEEP

It's wonderfully easy to lose yourself in the paintings of Else Bostelmann (1882–1961). The German-born Bostelmann painted watercolours of the fascinating deep-sea creatures that the American William Beebe (1877–1962) saw from his deep-sea submersible. Beebe, a biologist working for the New York Zoological Society, made his descents in the legendary Bathysphere, partnered by its inventor, American engineer Otis Barton. Bostelmann didn't go down in the Bathysphere herself; instead she based her drawings on descriptions dictated from the depths by Beebe via a telephone line. Between 1930 and 1934 the Bathysphere made thirty-five descents to the ocean floor off Bermuda, setting several world records for the deepest dives in the process.

In the United States, Beebe became a celebrity biologist. So passionate was he about marine life that he began to consider the possibility of underwater gardens for beach-front homes. In just a few days such a 'garden' would be filled with the most marvellous sea creatures, he thought. 'As birds collect about the luxuriant growths of a garden in the upper air, so hosts of fish will follow your labours, great crabs and starfish will creep thither, and now and then fairy jellyfish will throb past, superior in beauty to anything in the upper world, more delicate and graceful than any butterfly.'

A resident of New York, Beebe did not have an underwater garden himself. But his walls were covered with Bostelmann's watercolours.

>

Else Bostelmann (1882-1961) made live drawings of the deep sea creatures described by naval biologist William Beebe (1877-1962) via a telephone line from his submarine.

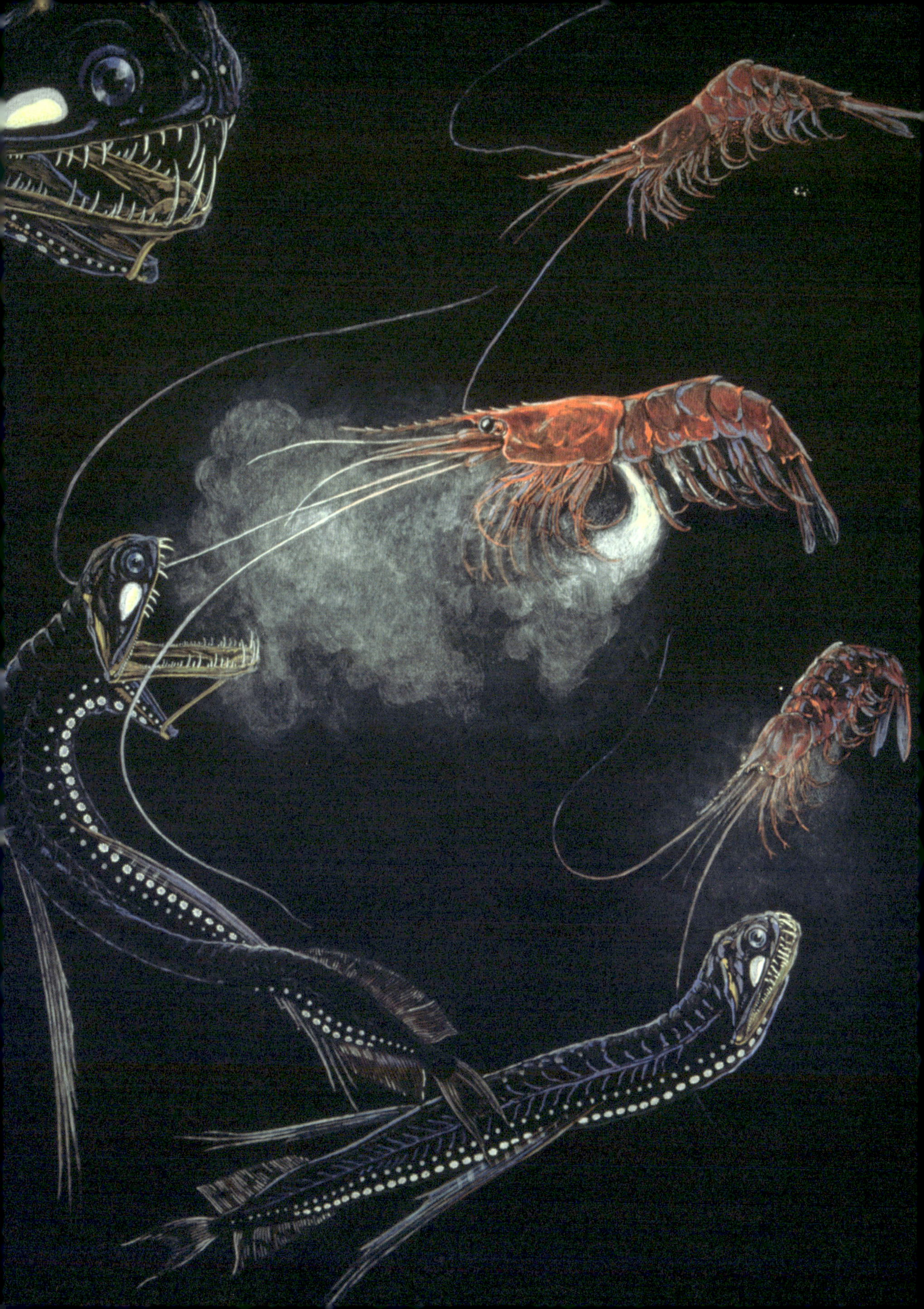

He dined on boiled toucan and rode on an alligator's back, or so the English eccentric and globetrotting taxidermist Charles Waterton (1782-1865) told his readers.

BOILED TOUCAN

Charles Waterton (1782–1865): English gentleman, eccentric, satirist, taxidermist, adventurer – in the nineteenth century few people would not have heard of him. His *Wanderings in South America, the North-West of the United States and the Antilles in the Years 1812, 1816, 1820 and 1824*, published in 1828, makes for extremely colourful reading. He recounts extraordinary anecdotes about his audacious exploits in the South-American jungle, such as the time he rode on an alligator's back. Or his conversations with insects. Or the time he offered his toe to a blood-drinking vampire bat.

But he's at his best when the topic turns to his taxidermic skill. It was while eating a boiled toucan, he tells us, that the best method of preserving the bird's brilliantly coloured bill suddenly occurred to him: hollow it out, coat it with gum arabic and chalk, and touch it up with paint. These were not idle words. Waterton was an innovative taxidermist with a highly accomplished technique.

He will probably be best remembered as an eccentric who criticized the political events of his day through the witty use of his preserved specimens, cleverly modelling his creatures so that the face of a famous politician could sometimes be discerned, for instance. Lampoons in the form of stuffed animals – a rare genre.

ANTHROPOPHOTOGRAPHY

Few expeditions were purely scientific in intent. Almost invariably there was an element of nationalist strategy or commercial reconnaissance as well. As a rule, the team of explorers would include a scientist, a draughtsman and a cartographer. But from the mid-nineteenth century they also employed the new medium of photography to document their missions. Images of plants, animals, people and landscapes were captured on the light-sensitive photographic plates. Often, the photographs ended up in the collections of anthropological museums, likewise a new phenomenon in the nineteenth century.

In the nineteenth century photography was often used in anthropological research.

I am not ashamed to confess that
since I have been in this land of America,
where everything to be seen – the way
of life of its inhabitants, the form of
the animals, what the Earth produces – is so
unlike what we have in Europe,
Asia and Africa that it may well be called
a 'New World'.

Jean de Léry, *History of a Voyage to the Land of Brazil*, 1578

<

'The rare and curious umbrella bird', a drawing from *The Naturalist on the River Amazons* (1863) by Henry Walter Bates (1825–1892).

HUMAN ZOO

Exotica reflect the way we look at tropical nature – and likewise at 'exotic' peoples. So we can compare, so we can make a distinction between 'us' and 'them'. In the nineteenth and early twentieth centuries, 'exotic' men and women were regularly seen as a spectacle, something to be stared at. This is certainly how native Americans from both the north and south of the continent were treated. They were shipped to Europe and housed in cages or mocked-up villages, purely as entertainment, just like wild animals in a zoo or exotic plants in a botanical hothouse. 'Exotic' people were exhibited in zoos, on markets and at world fairs. Sometimes such displays were even called 'human zoos'. This was ideal for the anthropologists of the time, who could photograph, measure or make plaster-casts of the 'natives' without the inconvenience of a hazardous expedition. The ostensible 'scientific' reason was to discover which race represented the 'missing link' between monkeys and man. For many Europeans, the human zoo was their first real encounter with people from Africa, Oceania or America. Shocking as it may seem now, at the time it was a fairly normal way of expressing white superiority.

—

'RED INDIAN' CLICHÉS

Native North Americans were always a highlight of these anthropo-shows. They were recruited from their reservations and paid to act as if they were 'at home'. It was all a sham, of course – there was scarcely a woman to be seen and their so-called authentic rituals were little more than a 'best of' compilation of clichés, with wigwams, feathered war bonnets, horses, peace pipes and totem poles.

Every conceivable stereotype was crammed into one commercial holdall in Buffalo Bill's Wild West Show. In 1883 William 'Buffalo Bill' Cody, an American buffalo hunter turned impresario, formed his own Indian attraction and for the next thirty years he toured with it through America and Europe. It was hugely successful, as were the books by the German author Karl May (1842–1912), who based his adventures of Winnetou and Old Shatterhand directly on Buffalo Bill's wild-west spectaculars.

>

The American impresario Buffalo Bill heaped cliché upon cliché in his touring Wild West shows.

>>

Tiki, collage of woodcut and monotype on canvas by Belgian contemporary artist Tom Liekens.

BUFFALO BILL'S
WILD WEST & ROUGH RIDERS
THE STROBRIDGE LITHO CO.
A TRIBE OF SIOUX INDIANS ON THE TRAIL LED BY CHIEF IRON TAIL

Chapter 3

OUT OF AFRICA

The Dark Continent. A Black Hole for Exotica?

—

But my estimates, for instance,
based upon book information,
were simply ridiculous,
fanciful images of African attractions
were soon dissipated,
anticipated pleasures
vanished, and all crude ideas
began to resolve themselves
into shape.

Henry Morton Stanley

—

<

Buffalos Driven to the Edge of the Chasm opposite Garden Island, Victoria Falls
by Thomas Baines (1820-1875), oil on canvas.

BUM AHOY!

If the first thing that springs to mind when you look at this *coco de mer* (*Lodoicea Seychellarum*) is a generous bottom, don't worry, you're not alone. No less a luminary than General Charles George Gordon wrote of it in 1881, 'Externally the *coco de mer* represents the heart, while the interior represents the belly and thighs, the true seat of carnal desires.' When Gordon (1833–1885) landed in the Seychelles in that year it seemed as if he had found the Garden of Eden, with the *coco de mer* as the forbidden fruit, especially as it grew only on female palms. In fact the suggestive fruit had been a talking point with many a cabinet of curiosities since the sixteenth century, not least because it was regarded as a powerful aphrodisiac. The nut was named the *coco de mer* or 'sea coconut' by mariners sailing the Indian Ocean who spotted it floating on the water. Usually, it was left in its natural state, but occasionally it would be halved or transformed into a functional object such as a drinking cup or box. Sometimes, if given to a goldsmith to embellish, parts would be gilded with gold or silver leaf. The nuts came from the Seychelles but reached western curiosity cabinets indirectly, in vessels from the East Indies that also shipped other sorts of exotica, such as silver or porcelain, via the Portuguese port of Goa on the west coast of India. The most famous example is in the Royal Danish Kunstkammer at Rosenborg Castle in Copenhagen, where it is described in the 1737 inventory as 'complete, rare and beautiful'.

—

UGLY 'ETHIOPIANS'

Are zebras black with white stripes? Or white with black stripes? Most African people regard zebras (correctly) as black animals with white stripes, states American palaeontologist Stephen Jay Gould (1941–2002) in his article 'How Did the Zebra Get its Stripes?' It's all a question of your point of view – something the fourteenth-century travel writer Sir John Mandeville had already discovered. He encouraged his readers to empathize with strange races by putting themselves in the minds of exotic people and imagining their reactions. The thirteenth-century French canon Jacques de Vitry also put the exotic in perspective in his *Historia Orientalis*, even if his phrasing is a little unfortunate. 'Just as we consider the pygmies dwarves,' he wrote, 'so they would judge us giants if they saw one of us among them ... We consider the black Ethiopians ugly, but among them, the blackest is judged the most beautiful.' The book was enormously popular, even more so than its predecessor, *Historia Occidentalis*, which had covered the west. And why? Because the exotic peoples, animals, places and wonderful scenes from the east – in which he included Ethiopia – contained in it were so fascinatingly described. Even though it was implicit propaganda for the crusades, the *Historia Orientalis* was noticeably milder in tone than the twelfth-century *Liber miraculorum* by the French monk Herbert of Clairvaux, whose description of demons also features the much-maligned 'Ethiopians': 'Demons ... resemble monstrous men, gigantic in stature, black like Ethiopians in skin colour, agile like serpents, ferocious like lions.' And who, then, could have told him any different?

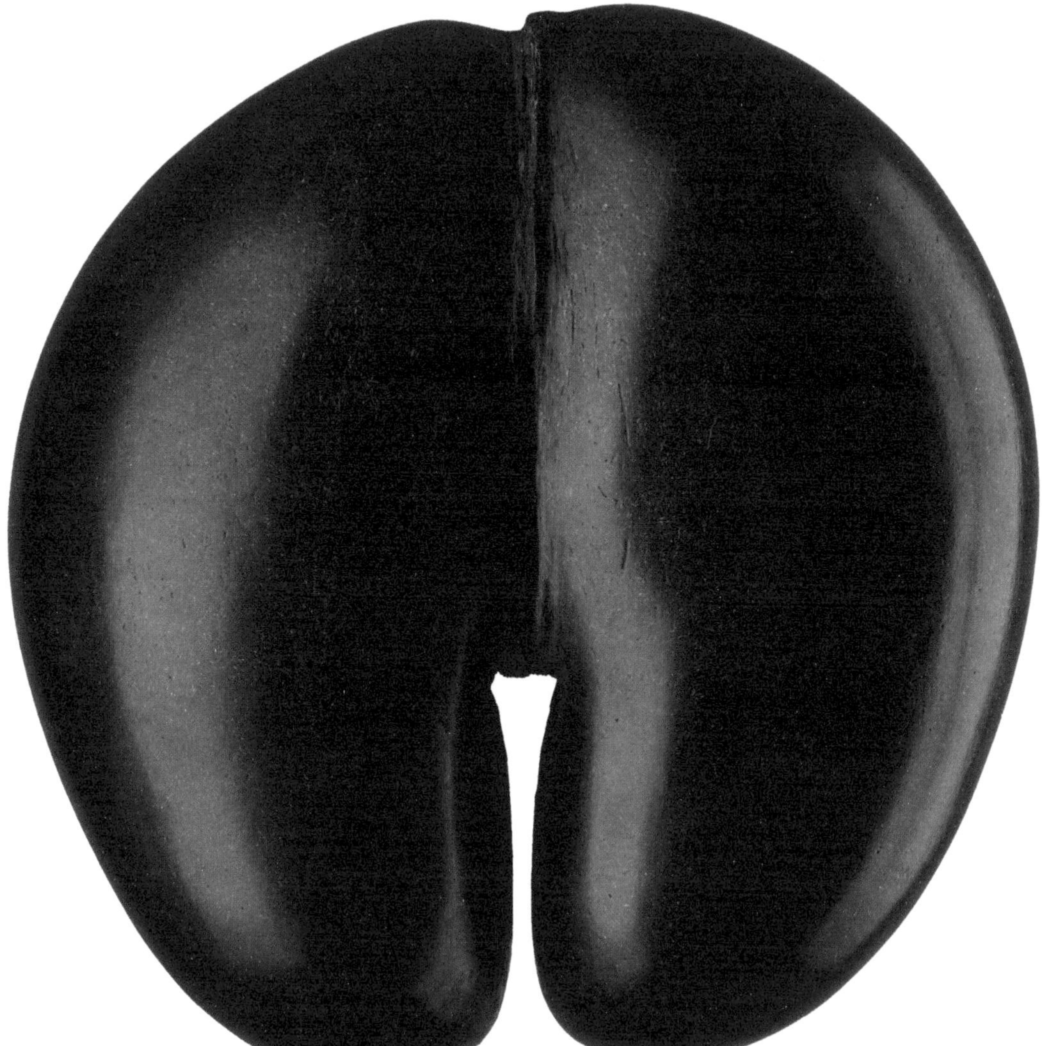

A suggestive curiosity: a *coco de mer* from the Seychelles.

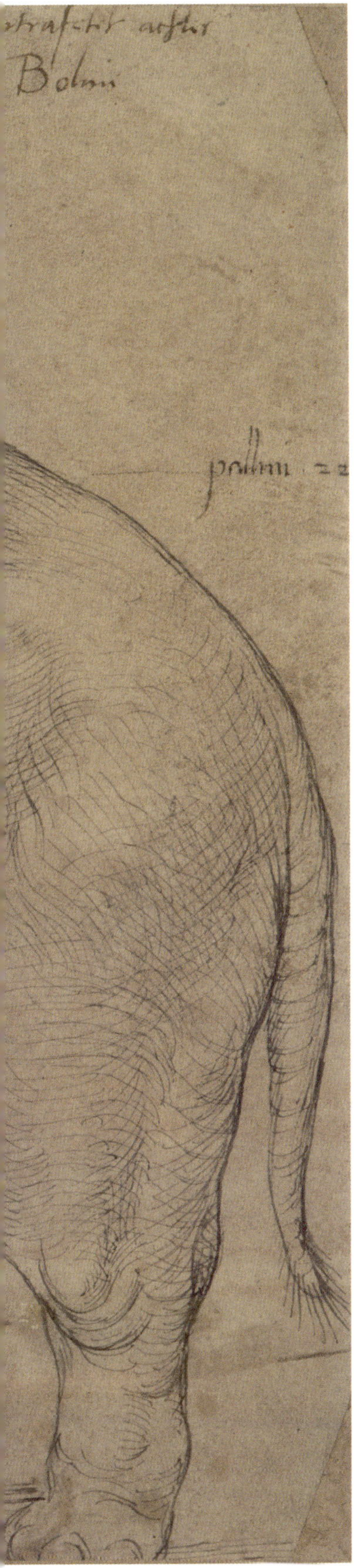

LEO AFRICANUS

Speaking of lions ... Leo Africanus, born al-Hasan ibn Muhammad al-Wazzan in Andalusia around 1494, was a highly educated Berber diplomat and writer whose travels took him to Algeria, Senegal, Sudan, Mali, Tunisia and Egypt. His magnum opus, entitled *Descrittione dell'Africa*, is a largely first-hand description of the geography of North Africa. In 1520 his life took a fateful turn when he was captured by pirates. Eventually, after a period of imprisonment, he was presented to Pope Leo X as a gift. From the pope, who welcomed his intellectual credentials, Hasan received baptism and the name Leo Africanus. His books on North Africa were standard works of reference for decades. Leo X, born Giovanni di Lorenzo de' Medici, was a great lover of exotica of all kinds and even had a pet white elephant named Hanno. Hanno, who died in 1516, had been sent by Manuel I of Portugal when Leo was elected to the papacy a couple of years earlier. It was certainly not unusual for popes to receive exotic gifts from foreign rulers. Nevertheless, the exhumation of elephant bones in the Vatican in 1962 caused some puzzlement, until a historian from the Smithsonian Institution reconstructed the story of Leo's pet. Hanno, it seems, came from Cochin in India, whence he was shipped via Lisbon to Italy. When Hanno was led into Rome a huge and astonished crowd gathered. As the pope said when he wrote to thank King Manuel, 'The sight of this quadruped provides us with the greatest amusement and has become for our people an object of extraordinary wonder.' Every weekend, the pope opened the newly built elephant house to the public. Eventually, Hanno died of constipation. Gold was administered as a remedy, but that only made the animal worse. The first elephant in Rome since the Roman Empire was a symbol of Portugal's colonial power, but also of the decadence of the papal court.

<

Hanno, the white elephant sent to Pope Leo X, a great lover of exotica.

<
Taxidermist, oil and acrylics on canvas by Belgian contemporary artist Tom Liekens.

EXTRA-LARGE EGGS

What were ostrich eggs doing dangling from the ceilings of medieval and Renaissance churches? It's hard to imagine, but some sources also mention whale skeletons, griffin claws and dried crocodiles being used as ecclesiastical interior decoration. And the purpose? To instil in the congregation awe of God's creation and power. Ostrich eggs have been in vogue since the Middle Ages, sometimes in their natural form but usually mounted as a cup or reliquary. In secular circles too, the ostrich was highly prized among collectors of exotica. John, Duke of Berry, and likewise the Florentine Strozzi family, had a live specimen. And the eggs became part of his curiosity cabinet, like those of many other collectors. They believed in the magical powers of the extra-large eggs. In powdered form, they thought they could even help to cure kidney problems and poisoning.

—

SCULPTURAL BILLS

One thing that was indispensable to the exotica section of every self-respecting curiosity cabinet was a swordfish bill. Most came from African waters, and ever since the Renaissance they topped the list of must-haves. That's partly because they have such sculptural quality, but especially because they looked like swords (with very sharp teeth). A fish in the form of a sword – it led collectors to philosophize about how nature had imitated man. Or was it the other way round?

A sawfish bill turned into a decorative sword.

<

A highly-prized ostrich egg cup, mounted in gold and coral.

Novelty excited wonder in persons
whose habits of thought are shaken
and disarranged by what they see.
But the element of wonder never lies
in the phenomenon or event observed,
but always in the person observing.

Ernst Mach, naturalist and philosopher, 1838-1916

<

A man from Kivu by the Belgian photographer Rosmant, 1945 1950.

TREE OF LIFE

No exotica collection was complete without its coral. Collectors were fascinated by coral because it fell between two stools: was it a plant or a mineral? Moreover, it was believed to have medicinal properties, being particularly effective against poison, so it was said. Hence coral spoons, used to mix medicine or test just how poisonous certain mixtures were. If the coral changed colour it was a sign that the substance was toxic. Coral also had a mythological connotation as a 'sea tree', from which all life originated. According to the Roman poet Ovid, coral was petrified seaweed, turned red by the blood that dripped from the severed head of Medusa the Gorgon, whose gaze could turn living beings to stone. That is why red coral is still used in amulets – to ward off the 'evil eye'.

—

A PARROT OF FLANDERS?

Adriaen Collaert (1560–1618), an engraver who worked for the artist Maarten de Vos and the Plantin-Moretus family of printers, specialized in animals. It was a canny decision on his part, for in his day exotic animals were eagerly collected, live, stuffed and in the form of prints. Explorers were responsible for this rage for exotic souvenirs, from shells to corals and birds. Around 1600, Collaert published three different animal albums about animals, birds and fish. This is an engraving from *Avium Vivae Icones*, the volume on birds. It shows a pair of African grey parrots. We see one from the back; the other is nibbling a large cherry. The birds are beautifully presented, but something seems slightly amiss, for they are perched on branches in a distinctly Flemish-looking landscape, which is certainly not their natural habitat. Collaert has used a touch of artistic licence. This species is mainly native to the African rainforest, though a number of wealthy collectors did have African greys as pets. They found the bird's capacity to memorize and repeat a surprisingly large vocabulary highly diverting.

An African parrot in a Flemish landscape: an exotic fantasy by Adriaan Collaert (1560-1618)

Pictures are all that remain of the extinct Mauritius pigeon.

MAURITIUS PIGEON

Lying in the Indian Ocean, to the east of Madagascar, is the island of Mauritius. To collectors of exotica, Mauritius was familiar ground: it was where the dodo peacefully roamed the forest floor – at least until the Dutch arrived and established a colony on the hitherto uninhabited island. The resulting disruption of the biotope was catastrophic for the endemic species. The Dutch slaughtered the giant tortoises, exhausted the local ebony, and introduced alien species such as goats, monkeys, rats and deer. The dodo, a flightless bird about the size of a swan which until then had had virtually no natural enemies, didn't stand a chance and was soon extinct. It was followed by the *pigeon hollandais* or Mauritius blue pigeon. That this bird should bear a French nickname is due to the French settlers who arrived on the island – which the Dutch had meanwhile abandoned as unprofitable – in 1721. The French biologist Pierre Sonnerat came up with *pigeon hollandais* in 1782, saying that the bird's colours reminded him of the Dutch flag. Just one living bird reached the Netherlands around 1790 and was kept in the private zoo of William V of Orange-Nassau. Tangible evidence that the Mauritius blue pigeon ever existed is incredibly rare. In the entire world there are only three mounted specimens. Back in Paris, Sonnerat deposited two pigeon skins in the Muséum nationale d'Histoire naturelle. A hundred years later, only one was left and that was in a very poor state, having been too enthusiastically fumigated in an attempt to kill parasites. However, depictions of the *pigeon hollandais* may still be found, such as this watercolour by G. Haasbroek, produced around 1790 for his *Iconographia Zoologica*.

—

HUMAN OR ANIMAL?

By the sixteenth century the African peoples encountered by European explorers were already being nicknamed. Accounts of them were unflattering and Eurocentric. For instance, the Khoikhoi or 'Hottentots' were described as 'a sort of hybrid of human and animal'. It was said of the Bushmen that 'in appearance they look more like apes than humans'. Native Americans were portrayed in a very uncomplimentary way, even by 'neutral' scholars and scientists. The British naval officer Robert FitzRoy (1805–1865) called the indigenous people of Tierra del Fuego, at the southernmost tip of Argentina, 'a mockery of humanity, whose women could only be called women out of courtesy'. FitzRoy was the captain of HMS *Beagle*, the ship on which Charles Darwin carried out research that led him to his theory of evolution. Darwin, too, was not particularly kind to the Yámana in Tierra del Fuego. 'I would not have believed how entire the difference between savage and civilized man is. It is greater than between a wild and domesticated animal', he noted. 'These poor wretches were stunted in their growth, their hideous faces bedaubed with white paint, their skins filthy and greasy, their hair entangled, their voices discordant and their gestures violent. Viewing such men one can hardly make oneself believe that they are fellow creatures and inhabitants of the same world.'

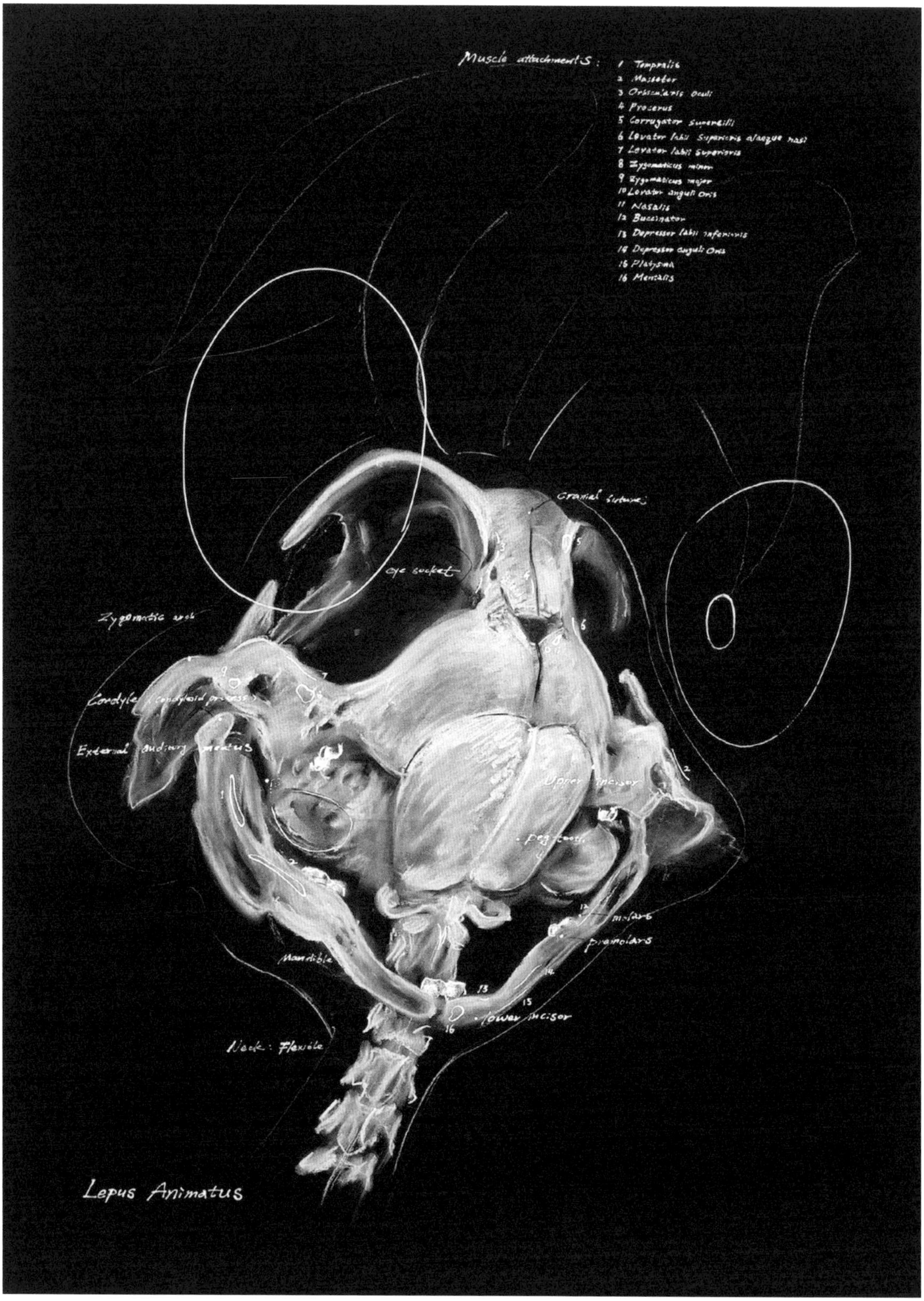

B08, a work by South Korean contemporary artist Hyungkoo Lee.

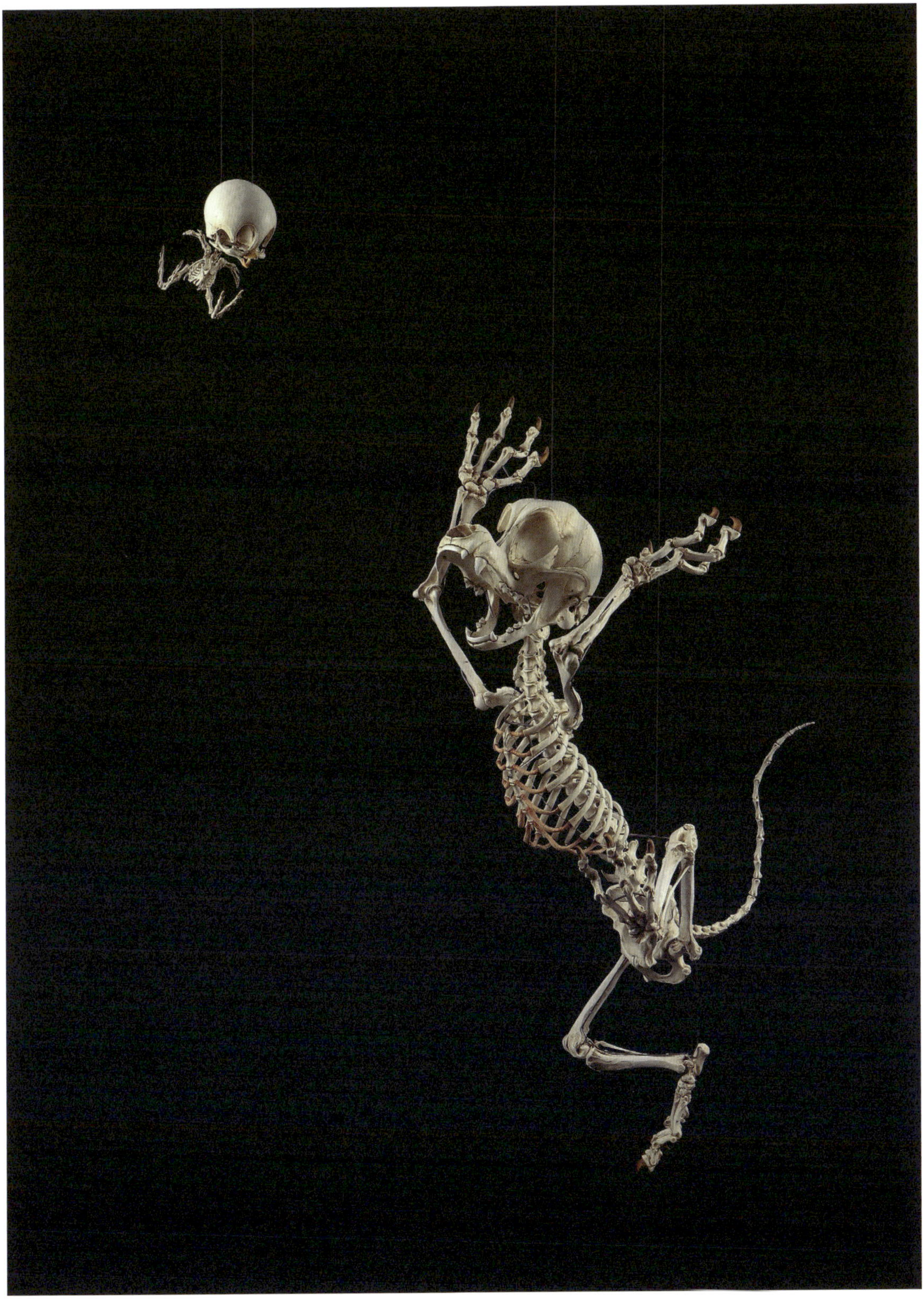

Felis Animatus & Leiothrix Lutea Animatus by South Korean contemporary artist Hyungkoo Lee.

HILARIOUS HYENAS

This picture of a hyena might raise a smile; nevertheless, the artist, explorer Robert Jacob Gordon (1743–1795), went about his task in earnest. This amateur naturalist – Dutch but of Scottish ancestry – rose to become commander of the Cape Colony in South Africa. He was a meticulous verbal and visual recorder of the fauna, flora and inhabitants of the Cape region, and the fact that he spoke a couple of the local languages, Xhosa and 'Hottentot', made the trips he undertook between 1777 and 1795 much easier than they might have been. His maps, letters and drawings, collectively known as the *Gordon Atlas*, have been rediscovered and are exceptionally well preserved. Some of his illustrations – in ink, pencil and watercolour – have holograph annotations, and sometimes even a date, giving them vivid authenticity. He drew this spotted hyena, known locally as a tiger wolf, on 17 July 1777. In a note he refers to the *stinkende muskuszak* or 'stinking musk bag' of this female hyena. He also mentions that in South Africa it's believed that the animal changes sex annually, being female one year, male the next. Gordon's plant drawings are also still impressive, 250 years after he put pencil to paper.

—

EGYPTOMANIA IN THE ZOO

The nineteenth century was the age of chinoiserie, japonism and Egyptian revival. Diverse archaeological discoveries and Napoleonic military campaigns had led to a new interest in Egypt. Africa's 'rediscovered' empire became the latest thing, and 'Egyptian' elements began to infiltrate European decorative and visual arts. Antwerp Zoo has boasted a 'neo-Egyptian' pavilion intended for African species since 1856. Painted all over with hieroglyphics and orientalist scenes, the building is a veritable temple. In the nineteenth century the first zoological gardens opened. Though some were established by learned bodies for scientific study, many were repurposed royal menageries. The zoos were symbols of colonial power, particularly when animals from a country's colonies were to be seen in them. Botanical gardens expressed the same kind of imperialist braggadocio; they were conceived as a kind of Garden of Eden, with exotic species from all over the globe. And it wasn't just fauna and flora that were put on show. In the nineteenth century, the 'spectacle' of exotic people – whether in a cage, museum or hut – also drew crowds of spectators. And just as some animals are less equal than others (to rephrase Orwell), not all peoples had reached an equal level of civilization. The races of man were still seen as a hierarchy. No prizes for guessing who was at the top of the pyramid: the western Europeans, of course.

>

Robert Jacob Gordon (1743-1795) drew this hilarious spotted hyena or 'tiger wolf' on 17 July 1777.

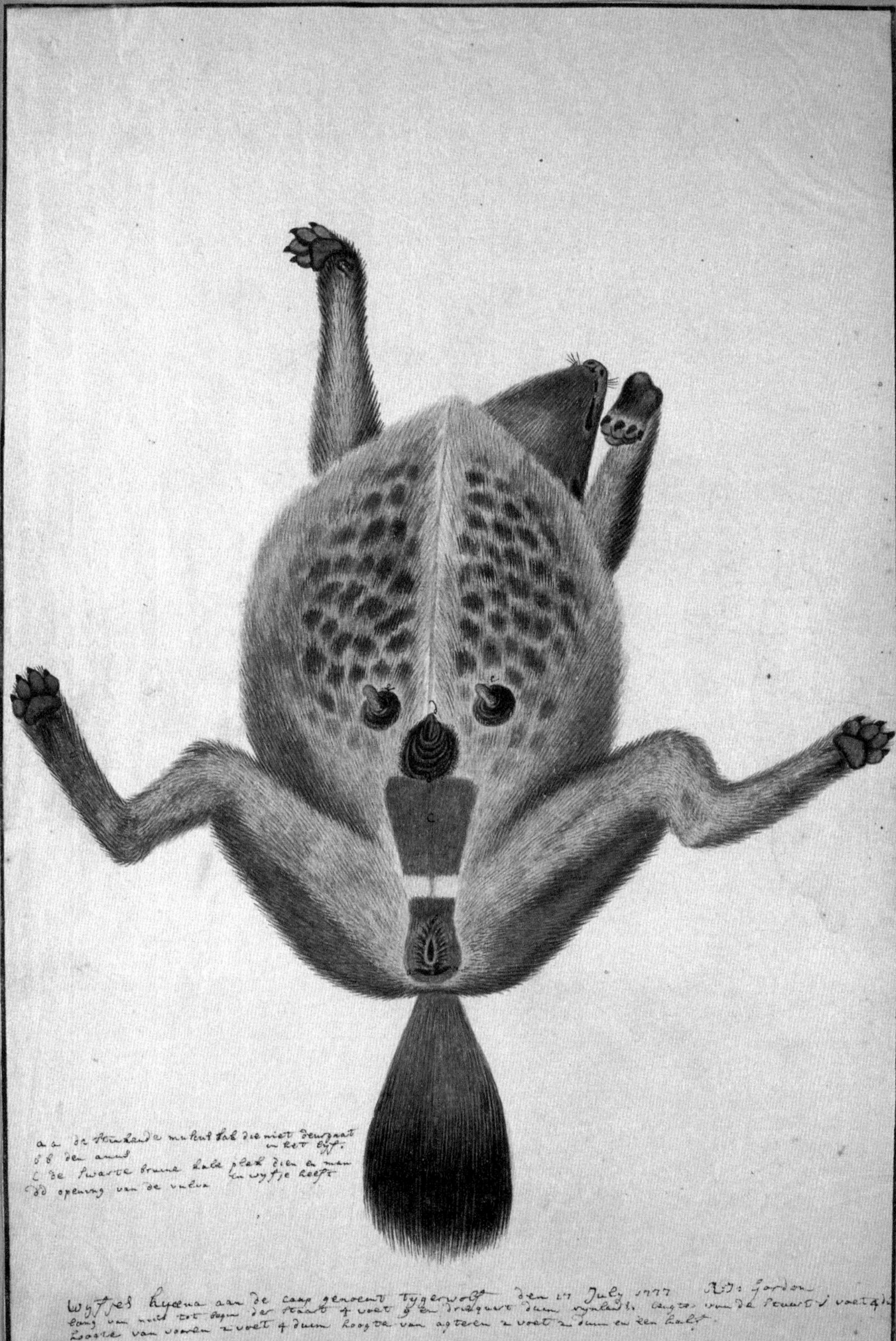
a a de stinkende mukus tak die niet deurgaat in het lyf.
b b den anus
c de swarte brune kale plek dien en man en wyfje heeft
d d opening van de vulva
Wyfjes hyæna aan de caap genoemt tygerwolf den 17 July 1777 R:J: Gordon
hoogte van voren 2 voet 4 duim hoogte van agteren 2 voet 2 duim en een half

A human zoo exhibition of the German zoo keeper and circus director Carl Hagenbeck in the 1930s.

EXOTIC ENTERTAINMENT

In the nineteenth century, as zoos, natural history museums and world fairs increased in number, exotica were also looked at in a different way, and by a different audience, becoming a form of live entertainment. Typical of that time was the travelling curiosity show – often dubbed a 'freak show' – where, in addition to exotic animals both living and stuffed, human beings were also exhibited. The Panoptikum run by Hermann Präuscher (1839–1896), a former lion tamer, in Vienna in 1872 was one such spectacle. Compare it to a touring sensation museum: the public paid money to see anatomical models, waxworks and ethnographic art. Sometimes the Panoptikum had live 'natives' on show too, perhaps from Africa or North America, arranged in a tableau vivant. Sometimes the human exotica were caged, sometimes displayed in a denigratory setting of counterfeit huts or tents. And just like the tropical animals in contemporary zoos, many of those people died of cold or hardship. By the mid-nineteenth century such travelling freak shows had become quite common. Had you been in Amsterdam in 1864, for example, you could have seen a 'tiger child from Bengal' as it 'suckled the teats of a Bengal tiger' found in the wild – so it was claimed. Every evening it was given live (!) chickens to eat. A few years earlier, in 1851, still in Amsterdam, 'South African dwarves' were on show – not an animal species but a human race that lived in holes in the ground. On their menu: snakes and locusts. Their job: to put on a performance while a presenter reeled off his spiel to the audience. Sometimes they acted out a fight, a tribal war or a marriage ritual. It's not unlike the way anthropomorphic taxidermists mounted animals in the late nineteenth century, as pets mimicking human actions – rabbits playing cards, rats getting married or mice reading books. The border between the (exotic) man and animal was blurred.

—

PEOPLE SHOWS OR 'HUMAN ZOOS'

Hermann Präuscher was not the only showman in town. There was also Carl Hagenbeck, a famous zoo owner and circus entrepreneur from Hamburg who was also an extremely successful dealer in exotic animals. Between 1874 and 1913, as interest in his animal park declined, he turned to displaying people. His first venture was with a family of Lapps (Sami), who arrived with their tents and sleds, and huskies and reindeer, and put on a show re-enacting daily life in Lapland. Hagenbeck called his spectacle a *Völkerschau* or 'people show'. He organized hundreds of them throughout Europe, in zoos, cities and circuses and at world fairs, though the way he treated his human exhibits was less than respectful. They were typecast as head-hunters, cannibals and benighted primitives – one name used was *die Gorilla-Neger vom Congo*. According to Hagenbeck, the ethnic groups he showed were less civilized than Europeans, which was the very thing to appeal to the paying public.

The border between exploration and exploitation became narrower and narrower. Over the years his audiences were treated to performances by Nubians, Eskimos, Fuegians, Kalmucks, Amazons, Indians, Ashanti, Samoans and other peoples. Perhaps his greatest success was the thrilling spectacle of 'wild Amazon women' from the kingdom of Dahomey (present-day Benin). Before the public's eyes a comely company of dusky maidens (the king of Dahomey's bodyguard), clad in shells and corals and little else, was transformed into a screaming blood-thirsty horde of 'wild monsters' as they demonstrated their martial skills. For the participants these performances were exhausting – ten hours a day in weather they were completely unused to. In 1880 an entire Eskimo family, brought to Germany for a people show, died. At the end of his life, Hagenbeck looked back at his career as an animal and people impresario. He wrote in melancholic mood: 'In my mind, the people exhibitions form a complete whole, rich in persons and events. How many dark heads from that time do I see again before me now, in my thoughts? Dark eyes in black or yellow faces, looking in astonishment and admiration at the incomprehensible wonders of the civilized world. Where are you all, you Africans, Indians, you red sons of the wilderness, you Eskimos and Laplanders, who trusted yourselves to my leadership in the land of those remarkable Whites, who gazed at you in crowds as if you were fabulous animals.'

OTA BENGA

Ota Benga. It's a name that conjures up both exoticism and racism, exoticism's ugly twin. In 1904 a young Congolese 'pygmy' named Ota Benga landed in America, destined for display at the world fair held in St Louis that year. His removal from what was then the Congo Free State, a vast tract of central Africa personally owned and exploited by Leopold I, King of the Belgians, had been orchestrated by the self-styled American explorer Samuel P. Verner, who had gone to Africa specifically to procure pygmies for the St Louis exhibition.

A couple of years later, Benga arrived at New York's Zoological Park in the Bronx, having been handed over to the zoo for keeping. 'Bushman Shares a Cage With Bronx Park Apes', read the somewhat controversial headline in the New York Times. Yet it was nothing less than the truth. From 10 September 1906 the young African lived in a cage in the New York zoo, occupying himself by weaving baskets, shooting arrows and playing with his pet parrot. The raucous crowds who flocked to see him found this highly amusing and arrived in ever-increasing droves. In that first September alone, 200,000 people came to gape at Ota Benga, who had meanwhile been transferred to a larger cage, which he shared with an orangutan. The exhibition of the 'pygmy' stole the headlines, but there was also a certain amount of political protest about Benga's melancholy and degrading fate. The zoological park's director, William Temple Hornaday, defended the exhibition, insisting that Benga was on show purely for ethnographic reasons, not as entertainment.

After considerable pressure, on Friday, 28 September Ota Benga was freed from the zoo. He was placed in an orphanage and later attended an African-American theological seminary. But gradually his disposition darkened and he was consumed by a longing to go home. On 19 March 1916, depressed and lonely, he shot himself.

As we've seen in the previous chapters, Europe also has a history of exhibiting 'exotic' peoples. In 1848, Antwerp's recently-founded zoo took delivery of an African slave, who came to be nicknamed 'Jefke'. On the left you'll see his portrait. The zoo's director, Jacques Kets, trained him up and gave him a job, and Jefke started work as a porter. He became a great favourite with the people of Antwerp. 'Jefke from the zoo' was himself an exotic attraction and drew extra visitors to the developing animal garden.

Cartoon of the South African 'Hottentot Venus', Saartjie Baartman (1770-1815), famed for her magnificent behind.

POOR SAARTJIE

The story of Saartjie Baartman (1770–1815), better known as 'The Hottentot Venus', is also typical. In the nineteenth century no people show was complete without a 'Hottentot'. Audiences loved them. But the Africans themselves were treated with a lack of respect that is now quite shocking. The programme from a Dutch people show describes their language as 'something that resembles the unpleasant scratching of a steam engine'. What happened to Saartjie Baartman demonstrated even less respect. Saartjie, a Khosian woman of the Cape Colony, was employed as a servant by a mixed-race entrepreneur, Hendrik Cesars. Through the scheming of Cesars and a British Army medical officer named William Dunlop who dabbled in human trafficking on the side, she ended up in Europe. In England, Dunlop and Cesars aimed to exhibit their 'Hottentot Venus', whose bottom was 'unequalled by any to be seen in London', in a people show. Their motives were purely financial. From 1810 Saartjie was put on show in various places in England; in 1814 she was also displayed in France. At the Palais Royal in Paris she was required to pose for scholars such as the naturalist Georges Cuvier, who wanted to record her particular physique in anatomical prints. Scientists deduced from her elongated labia that she was 'sexually voracious'. The cartoon of Saartjie now in the Teylers Museum in Haarlem says it all. Her sexual organs were preserved in alcohol after her death. And until 1976 the plaster cast of her body stood in the Museum national d'Histoire naturelle in Paris. In 2002, Saartjie Baartman's remains were returned to South Africa and finally laid to rest.

COME AND LOOK!

Like Hermann Präuscher's Panoptikum and Carl Hagenbeck's *Völkerschauen*, world fairs – typically nineteenth-century – were entertaining events that were also intended to showcase western colonial power. Such exhibitions were expressions of industrialization, technological progress and colonialism. At the Paris Exposition Universelle in 1867, there was for the first time a separate section with specific pavilions for exotic countries. This was a form of colonial propaganda, of course, with 'real' people and 'real' tableaux – sometimes even with complete villages or markets. There was no lack of exotic imagination; you could see an Arabic coffee house, a mosque and a nomads' tent complete with a fakir. At the Paris Exposition Universelle of 1889, the year that saw the unveiling of the Eiffel Tower (*the* French symbol of industrial progress), colonial villages were built as well. If you took a stroll along the Seine you could see the (fake) huts and the natives living in them. They sang, cooked food, made music and entertained the people ambling through the fair. The Exposition Internationale held in Antwerp in 1885 had twelve black Congolese on show. Visitors threw peanuts into their 'huts'. Three and a half million people came to see the 'Negro Village', an astonishing number. In 1895 Antwerp sought to do better still, displaying some 150 Congolese. But the Exposition Internationale de Bruxelles in 1897 outdid them both, for in that year there were 269 Congolese to be seen. It was this exhibition that inspired Leopold II, king of the Belgians, to build his Musée du Congo in Tervuren, an ethnographic museum that also underlined colonial pride.

>
World fairs were showcases for colonial power.

Vignette for a map of Africa by Jan Luyken (1720-1772).

I. dos Picos
TROPIQUE DU CAPR
RIQUE

EPIMACHUS SPECIOSUS.

J. Gould & W. Hart, del. et lith.

Walter Imp.

Chapter 4

THE RAREST THAT ASIA CAN PROVIDE

Exotica from One Thousand and One Nights

—

The country produces a diversity of beasts different from those of all the rest of the world. There are black lions with no other colour or mark. There are parrots of many kinds. Some are entirely white – as white as snow – with feet and beaks of scarlet. Others are scarlet and blue – there is no lovelier sight than these in the world. ... Then there are peacocks of another sort than ours and much bigger and handsomer. What more need I say? Everything there is different from what it is with us and excels in both size and beauty.

Marco Polo (1254-1324) on Quilon,
then one of India's foremost trading ports

—

<

Illustration of a bird of paradise, John Gould.

SUPPLY AND DEMAND

The earliest objects to be found in cabinets of curiosity came from Asia. There were already close contacts with that part of the world via the Silk Road when the first medieval collections began to be assembled. The accounts brought back by travellers and explorers enabled Europeans to form a picture of that continent. Marco Polo (1254–1324) made several journeys to Asia in the late thirteenth century. His *Travels* transported Europeans to Asia. Not physically, of course. Very few could journey to such distant realms in reality. But the extraordinary tales encouraged a new sort of crusade – a quest for the rarest exotica Asia could provide. At the end of the fifteenth century the Portuguese explorer Vasco da Gama (1460 –1524) rounded the Cape of Good Hope and found a sea route to India. Soon, there were new maritime trade routes to Indonesia, China and Japan as well. And, for a long time, Asia was the focus of maritime trade. From its ports huge quantities of exotic herbs, ores, diamonds, textiles, porcelain, pearls and much more were exported to Europe. This was good news for dealers and collectors, who could thus enhance their collections with exotic items. Colonial trade was not all one way. In Asian ports, where many exotica were traded, local craftsmen spotted an opportunity. Well aware of the rising demand for exotic novelties, they themselves began to create objects deliberately designed to appeal to collectors. Sometimes they turned a natural object into a luxury item – a piece of coral into a spoon, for instance, or a nautilus shell into a silver-mounted drinking cup. 'Kraak ware', which from the late sixteenth century was manufactured specifically for export to Europe, is a classic example. It spawned imitations in the west, most notably the blue-and-white pottery known as Delft Blue, made in and around Delft in the Netherlands, which was a cheaper alternative to the exorbitantly priced blue-and-white Chinese porcelain.

—

RHINOCEROS

Nothing brought a collection more status and renown than an exotic creature that lived and breathed, though few could afford such a thing. Live exotic animals were pretty much the preserve of princes and political or religious grandees. More 'ordinary' collectors of exotica, who lacked the money (or space) to keep a live rhino or elephant, had to be content with buying bits of them, objects made of rhinoceros horn or elephant ivory. In the Renaissance an elephant tusk was worth its weight in gold. Rhinoceros horns, like corals and bezoars (a small hard ball of indigestible matter formed in an animal's stomach), could be used as a natural remedy for poisoning. If you wanted to check whether poison had been slipped into your wine, for example, you first poured it into a goblet fashioned from rhino horn. If poison was present there would be a chemical reaction. As the German mystic Hildegard of Bingen, writing in the early twelfth century, assured her readers, a hot drink containing poison would bubble in the cup, whereas a cold drink would start to smoke. Fantastical? Maybe. But belief in the antidotal properties of rhino horn still lingers today. In the form of scrapings or powder it's very popular as a remedy for gout or fever. That explains why, sadly, the rhino is such a target for poachers.

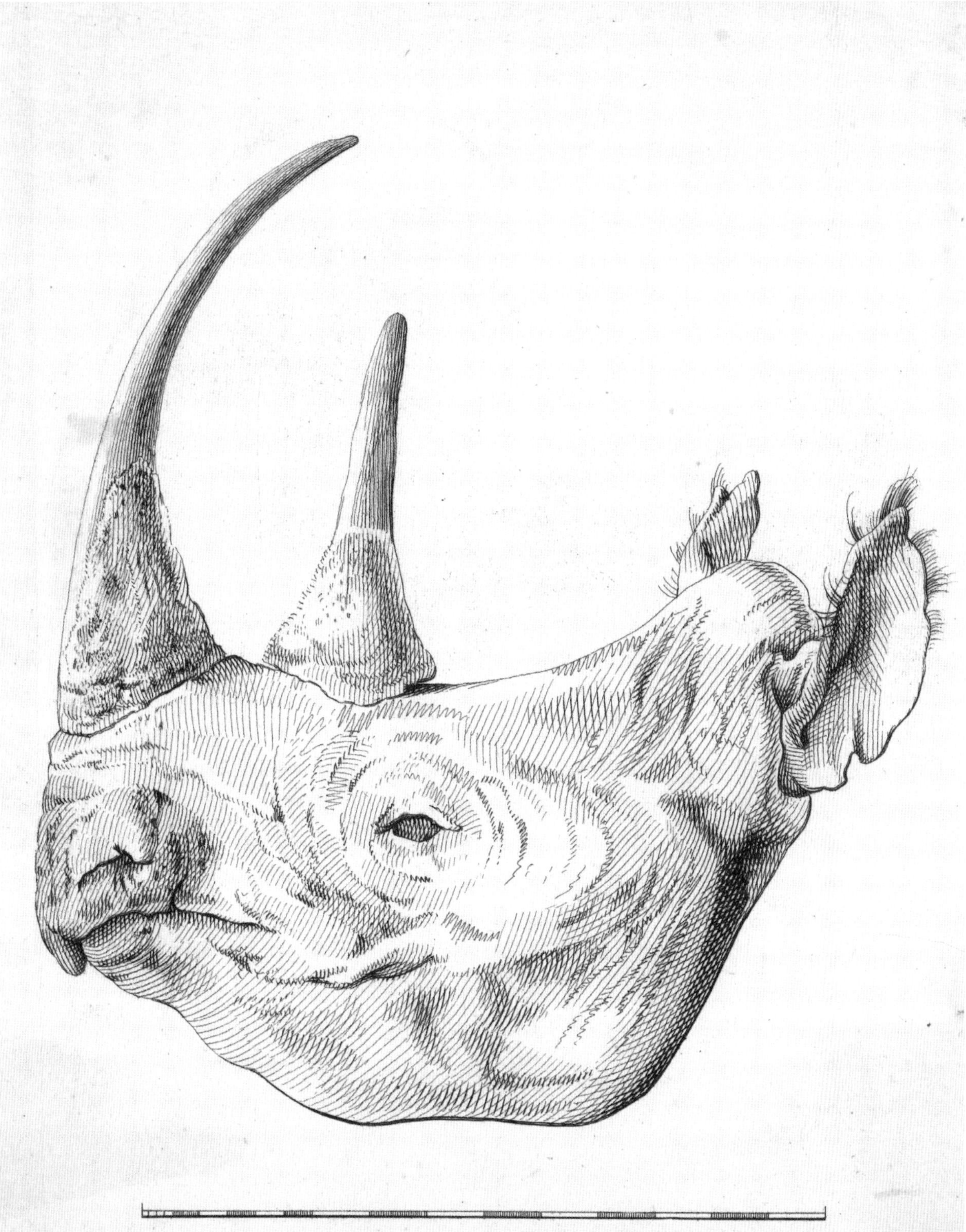

Head of a rhinoceros, Petrus Camper, 1737-1789.

LEGLESS BIRDS OF PARADISE

Another item which a collector of exotica would give practically anything to possess was a mounted bird of paradise. The first skins arrived in Europe in 1522, brought by explorers. The birds were called *manucodiata*, 'the birds of God', for it was thought that they had neither legs nor wings. The Italian gentleman-adventurer Antonio Pigafetta (1491–1534), who sailed with Magellan on his flagship the *Trinidad* and kept a detailed journal, noted that they did have legs, which were 'a palm in length and as thin as a reed'. Nobody credited that. 'Only unbelievers dare to state that they have legs', declared one of the sixteenth century's most famous naturalists, Ulisse Aldrovandi (1522–1605). His book *Ornithologiae* (1599) was even to be found in Rubens's library. Some reference works of that time depict the bird of paradise floating gently among the clouds, living only on drops of descending dew. It was believed that they never landed, not even to breed; instead, the female laid her egg in a special cavity on the male's back. Perpetually in flight, they obviously didn't need legs. Only in death, when they fell from the sky, did they touch Earth for the first time. Carl Linnaeus (1707–1778), the Swedish founder of the classification system for animals, plants and minerals, described it in 1758 as the 'footless bird of paradise'. Indeed, right up until the end of the eighteenth century there was complete confusion over the legs of birds of paradise – even though by then there were specimens that unquestionably possessed legs and feet. It was food for discussion among collectors and zoologists – which only made the bird of paradise even more desirable.

—

SUPPING FROM A SHELL SPOON?

The way a seventeenth-century craftsman has transmogrified this Asian tiger cowrie into a spoon is stunning. Whether much soup was supped with it, we can only wonder. But there is no doubt that this object was intended for the European market. Their graphic patterning and porcelain shine made cowries desirable in themselves. But, as we see from this one, they were also carved into cutlery – a fate that befell other naturalia at the hands of skilled craftsmen; corals became handles, lobster claws became perfume boxes. In fact, lobsters were regarded as monsters, reputedly able to pierce right through anyone who tried to catch them, according to the *Museum museorum* by the German collector, Michael Bernhard Valentini, published in 1714 and describing plants, minerals, fossils, shells and other natural wonders. That is why large claws were worth huge amounts of money: giant lobsters were almost impossible to catch. The largest claws were allowed to remain in their natural state; others were fashioned into flasks or boxes, for perfume for instance. Complete tortoise shells were also turned into similar luxury accessories. In the late sixteenth century the Indo-Portuguese province of Gujarat was famed for its tortoiseshell workshops. Their exquisite objects were bought by Portuguese merchants and shipped to Lisbon, and from there they entered many a European private collection, including that of Catherine of Austria, queen of Portugal (1507–1578): she had twenty-two objects made of tortoiseshell.

Tortoise shells were so valuable that they were made into luxury items.

NATURE VERSUS CULTURE

Of all the shells thought worthy of inclusion in a curiosity cabinet, the nautilus was the most sought after by Renaissance exotica collectors. Found only in the tropical waters of the Pacific and Indian Oceans, the nautilus made its way into European collections via ports and mercantile centres. Sometimes it would still be in its natural form, but many were already mounted on a gold or silver foot. Very rarely, a shell would arrive that was entirely covered with scenes delicately carved in relief. In the Indo-Portuguese province of Gujarat, for example, from the seventeenth century, workshops specialized in working mother-of-pearl and shells of all kinds, specifically for the European market. Local craftsmen produced powder flasks, jewellery boxes, dishes and caskets that sold for considerable sums in Europe. Basically, they larded fairly common naturalia with conspicuous extravagance. Those lavish objects erased the boundary between nature and art. Is nature a work of art? Or had man raised nature's art to a higher level? Where, then, did the most *fantasia* reside: in the mind of the craftsman or in nature? That was the kind of dilemma created by the artificialia in European chambers of wonders.

<

An eye-wateringly expensive nautilus shell,
turned into an even dearer object of desire for collectors.

THE PRECIOUS WENTLETRAP

On an April day in 1762, the collection of Willem Baart, secretary of the Haarlem court and passionate collector, went under the hammer. In the auction catalogue we read: '*Laade 1, waar in leggen wenteltrappen en admiraalen van veelderley soorten, waar onder zijn extra rare'. Lot 1: een extra fraaije en compleete wenteltrap, groot 2 ¼ duim, waarvan nergens geen weerga gevonden is.* (Drawer 1, in which are wentletraps and admirals of various sorts, including exceptionally rare ones. Lot 1: an exceptionally fine and complete wentletrap, 2¼ thumbs in size, whose equal is not to be found.)' The 'precious wentletrap' (*Epitonium scalare*) is a sea snail with a spiral shell that has distinctive ribs, found between Japan and Australia. It is not a large shell, measuring between 3.5 and 7.5 cm, and its first appearance in European collections did not occur until 1650. Until well into the eighteenth century, it was thought to be extremely rare, and demand far exceeded supply. That of course had an influence on the price. Willem Baart's precious wentletrap was auctioned for 545 guilders, which at the time was twice what the average worker earned in a year. It's thought that Ferdinand I, holy Roman emperor (1503–1564), once paid 4000 guilders for a single precious wentletrap. The eighteenth-century Swedish biologist Carl Linnaeus (1707–1778) rightly regarded it as the most expensive species of shell. Given that it was so hard to come by, it's not surprising that pictures of the rare shell were also collectible, which brings us straight to the German Johann Gustav Hoch (1726–1779). His watercolour drawings of shells really are little gems – almost literally. They gleam like freshwater pearls, their lustrous surfaces subtly reflecting the windows of Hoch's workshop – a trick he borrowed from the painters of the Dutch Golden Age.

This fine sheet depicting shells, in watercolour on vellum, for sale by Daxer & Marschall at TEFAF Maastricht in 2017, is by the French natural scientist François Jean-Baptiste Ménard de la Groye (1775–1827). This drawing dates from the period 1807–1826 and was reproduced in Jean-Charles Chenu's important work of 1842 on shells and fossils, entitled: *Illustrations conchyliologiques ou description et figures de toutes les coquilles connues vivantes et fossiles, classées suivant le système de Lamarck modifié d'après les progrès de la science et comprenant les genres nouveaux et les espèces récemment découvertes.*

—

IMPROVING ON NATURE

On 2 February 1696 this extraordinary advertisement appeared in an Amsterdam newspaper: 'Cornelis Bellekin, artist, has invented an instrument enabling him to bore into diamonds, pearls, agates & c. in as thorough a manner as has ever been practised; he improves, amongst other things, all pearls exhibiting yellow or impure films or large holes; he makes them purer and reduces their cavities, polishes all manner of sea denizen and red coral, and also modifies delicate East Indian rarities and cabinets of all types, and carves, amongst other things, likenesses on mother-of-pearl, amber and red coral and all manner of histories on various

Artists like Cornelis Bellekin (1625-*c.*1710) improved on nature with their engraved shells.

materials, on exterior as well as interior surfaces; he resides in Koestraat, at the horse-pond house in Amsterdam.' Cornelis Bellekin (1625–*c.*1710) was then the most renowned specialist in polishing, sculpting and engraving shells, mother-of-pearl and minerals, most of which came from Asia. Specimens of his artistry were acquired for large sums by collectors such as Albertus Seba (1665–1736). In Seba's 1758 *Thesaurus* are nautiluses both natural and polished, and engraved by Bellekin. As we saw in Chapter 1, in 1717 Seba sold his shell cabinet, with its seventy-two drawers of specimens, to Tsar Peter the Great (1672–1725).

Some shell catalogues were hyper-realistic works of art in themselves. Left, by Johann Gustav Hoch (1726-1779), right, by Jean-Baptiste Ménard de la Groye (1742-1813).

A bezoar is a hard ball of indigestible matter that remains in an animal's stomach.
Thought to have magical properties, these 'stones' were avidly collected.

STONES FROM GOA

The proper name for this intestinal concretion is an enterolite. Use that word in the Middle Ages and all you'd get is a blank look. Talk about a bezoar, though, and all would become clear. Whatever you call it, the object in question is a hard ball or 'stone' of indigestible matter such as plant fibre or hair that stays in an animal's gut.

In fact a bezoar is a syndrome, but that was not how medieval man saw it. He believed a bezoar had therapeutic power; like coral or rhino horn, it was regarded as a remedy for all manner of ills. The word 'bezoar' comes from Persian and literally means 'protection from poison'. The stones were originally found in the stomachs of a type of Asian goat. Harry Potter fans know the word, of course, as bezoars are used in the books and films that feature him as an antidote to toxic potions. But centuries before Harry arrived at Hogwarts, bezoars were being collected as curiosities. To turn them into real luxury objects, they were sometimes encased in exquisite containers made of precious metals. Or you might hang your bezoar on a chain so you could dip it in water or wine as a pre-emptive antidote.

Many bezoars were imported from Goa, via Portuguese intermediaries. Because natural specimens were rare, a shrewd Jesuit named Gaspar Antonio devised a solution to that. Antonio worked as an apothecary in Goa and therefore had knowledge of all kinds of medicinal preparations. He developed a top-secret process for producing artificial bezoars. His recipe was a mixture of unicorn horn (actually the 'tusk' of a narwhal), amber, red and white coral, emerald powder, crushed pearls, earth, clay, musk and genuine bezoar. The resulting paste was rolled into little balls, which he then sold as a remedy for fever, leprosy, anaemia and blindness. He called his surrogate Pedra Cordial or Pedra de Goa. Natural and synthetic bezoars were worth more than their weight in gold – a fact that did the wily Antonio no harm at all, according to an account by the English mariner John Fryer, who between 1672 and 1681 passed by the Jesuit's thriving pharmacy several times.

—

MERCHANDISE

A collection of tropical objects or animals was a kind of world trip for armchair travellers. The richer the collector, the more exotic 'souvenirs' he could buy, and the more he 'knew' about the New World. But how did collectors in the Middle Ages and Renaissance come by their exotica? Where did they buy their exotic objects or animals? What was the missing link between those owners of *Wunderkammern* and that unknown New World? Who was responsible for supplies from Europe and Africa, Asia and America? Were specialist shops – such as today's Finch & Co. in London, Kunstkammer Georg Laue in Munich and Porfirius Kunstkammer in Neerijse in Belgium – already in existence? Well, yes, they were. In sixteenth-century travelogues, for example, Lisbon is described as *the* place to find luxury goods, wildlife and exotica from Asia and the Americas. Alongside all these were textiles and diamonds from India, ivory and crystal from Ceylon, pearls from Hormuz, mounted coconuts and shells, lacquered furniture from China and Japan, caskets in mother-of-pearl and tortoiseshell from Gujarat, and live turkeys from the New World.

—

BROKERS

The flow of luxury goods, such as shells or rare minerals, from overseas into port-cum-trading-centre cities that included Lisbon, Venice, Genoa, Antwerp, Valencia and Seville was guaranteed. But did the noble and princely collectors themselves go exotica-shopping in these places? Probably not. They had their advisers who presented objects they thought would appeal, just as today's art advisers keep an eye open and an ear to the ground on their clients' behalf. Royal collectors had their suppliers, dealers and agents – travelling merchants who acted as intermediaries. They sold on exotica, or searched for specific items for wealthy patrons. Their role was that of brokers; they were the channel through which the most sought-after objects were obtained. While the collectors received the compliments and applause, others were the silent suppliers of exotica and related luxury items.

N°5.
N°6.
N°7.
N°8.
N°9.
N°10.
N°11.
N°12.
N°13.
N°14.
N°15.
N°16.
N°17.
N°18.
Pinac. 8.
Pinac. 9.

A collection is a fleeting vehicle
similar to the seashore,
continuously changing and elusive
due to the movement of the waves.

Leon Battista Alberti (1404–1472), Italian humanist

<

Engraving of Levinus Vincent's *Wunderkammer* published in 1719.

Duke Albert V of Bavaria with a Lion, painting by Hans Mielich (1556).

A piece of coral mounted on a pedestal: decorative, curious and exotic.

MEYTING

Some of those agents were more than mere middlemen, they were real arbiters of taste. They were able to start a craze and make this or that curiosity highly desirable. They dealt in 'must-haves' for collectors who in many cases had unlimited budgets. Take Anthonio Meyting (1524–1591), a merchant from Augsburg. His was the brain behind the curiosity cabinets of Albert V of Bavaria (1528–1579) and Philip II of Spain (1527–1598). Research has shown that many exotica in *Wunderkammern* in Lisbon, Vienna, Prague, Madrid and Munich passed through his hands at some stage.

Meyting began his career with the Fuggers, the famous Augsburg banking family. Handily bilingual, he shuttled back and forth between the royal courts in Munich and Madrid, becoming a confidant of both Philip and Albert, who also used him to send gifts to each other. Between 1558 and 1579, for example, he bought for the court in Munich lemon trees for the palace gardens, woven mats from Asia, painted textiles from India, and a Mexican 'painting' made of parrot feathers. Albert V gave him a kind of roving commission to hunt for rare exotica in Spain. He built up an enormous network of informants and tipsters who helped him to secure the latest exotic must-haves.

LION ENCLOSURE AND PARROT CAGE

Emperor Rudolf II (1552–1612), archduke of Austria, had an enormous art collection, a vast *Wunderkammer* and several private zoos. Next to his castle, for instance, he had a lion enclosure that housed leopards and bears as well. He also had a pheasant garden, a lake full of tropical fish, and an aviary built in 1593. Eight years later, his parrot cage was also finished. At the time, parrots were still seen as 'birds from Asia', which is how they're described in the painted inventory of his collection, known as his *Bestiarium*. Rudolf commissioned some of the best artists of the day to work on his bestiary, including the specialists Joris Hoefnaegel and Roelant Savery. The result may still be seen today in the Austrian National Library in Vienna.

—

CHARCOAL EATER

An emu can swallow an apple as big as a fist. And it can eat hot charcoal without any problem. Or so the German doctor and collector Michael Bernhard Valentini (1657–1729) surmised in 1714 when striving to find some way of explaining the bird's large dark eggs. Emus and their huge dark-green eggs were incredibly rare in Europe. That naturally made them particularly desirable in the cabinets of curiosity of the Renaissance and Baroque. After the ostrich, the emu is the world's largest flightless bird. It's become Australia's unofficial national emblem. The first living specimen was seen in Europe in 1548, when a Dutch ship brought one from South-East Asia. At the time, it was called the New Holland casuaris. Mounted emu eggs were much more prestigious than ostrich eggs. Decorated with silver, gold or coral, they were used as drinking cups. And like many exotic must-haves, they were believed to have medicinal properties.

—

POSTHUMOUS REHABILITATION

'On 15 June in the year 1702, on the island of Ambon, there died an old man named Georg Everhard Rumphius who had spent half a century beneath the tropical sun and whose last years were consumed with a single longing. A longing for the publication of a twelve-volume work on which he had laboured for many years, about the flora of that island and the islands surrounding it.' The title of that mammoth work was *Het Ambonsch Kruidboek en de Ambonsche Rariteitkamer, over schaal- en schelpdieren van de Molukse wateren en de mineralen van de Indische Archipel* (*The Ambonese Herbal and the Ambonese Cabinet of Curiosities, on Crustaceans and Shellfish of the Moluccan Waters and the Minerals of the Indonesian Archipelago*). In his lifetime Rumphius never saw his hope fulfilled. Friends undertook the publication of the *Cabinet of Curiosities*, which appeared three years after its author's death. The *Herbal* had to wait another forty years. As for a biography of that remarkable man, nearly 250 years went by before one appeared. The introduction to *Rumphius, the Blind Seer of Ambon* is a movingly written rehabilitation of a forgotten Dutch–German

Georg Eberhard Rumphius (1627-1702), the blind naturalist of Ambon.

naturalist whose sudden blindness was only one of many tragedies to befall him. Yet throughout his life he remained a faithful employee of the Dutch East India Company, even when his lack of sight made his research difficult. 'No one has taken the trouble to tell how Rumphius died. Did he allow the years of his youth to pass before him one last time and call up the memories of his father and mother? In his final hours was he homesick for his native soil or for Holland, his second homeland, that he had served so faithfully and selflessly for fifty long years? Who stood at his deathbed to light his last moments? Did no one on Ambon realize that when Rumphius departed this life there passed away a scholar whose name would live on to the end of days? A man who was so far ahead of his time that in the entire eighteenth century no one would appear to continue his work? In Holland his death went unnoticed. The name Rumphius was remembered when the *Cabinet of Curiosities* was published, and many years later the *Herbal*.'

American snowy egret from the collection of the Western Foundation of Vertebrate Zoology in California, picture by American contemporary artist and photographer Rosamond Purcell. (original image is horizontal)

WONDERS FROM THE HIMALAYAS

No book about exotica would be complete without a mention of John Gould (1804–1881). Gould started life as a trainee gardener in the Royal Gardens at Windsor. But only a few years later he set himself up as a taxidermist specializing in birds. He was remarkably skilful, and it was not long before he was head-hunted by the Zoological Society in London, where, thanks to his encyclopedic knowledge of birds, he became curator of the bird section. One day a collection of birds from the Himalayas arrived. Many were unknown; most had never been described before. Like John Audubon with his *Birds of America* (see Chapter 2), Gould wanted to produce a book about these rare creatures. He possessed a sound business sense, and though, with its eighty hand-tinted plates, *A Century of Birds from the Himalaya Mountains* was expensive to produce, it still turned a handsome profit. John Audubon and Leopold I, King of the Belgians, were among those who signed up for a copy. This and subsequent publishing ventures proved so successful that they enabled Gould to go to Australia, to find and draw unknown antipodean species. As usual, his wife Elizabeth went with him. Gould produced rough sketches from which Elizabeth created the lithographic plates.

—

GHOSTBUSTING MUSHROOM

Also from the Himalayas are these ritual mist masks. They're made from a *lingzhi* fungus (*Ganoderma lucidum*), one of the oldest mushrooms in the world to be used therapeutically and part of traditional Chinese medicine for over two thousand years. Buddhists use fungus masks like this to drive away malevolent spirits that dwell in the mountain mist. The art lies in seeing facial features in the natural form of the mushroom. Rudimentary eyes and mouth are cut out, so the mushroom resembles a wrinkled face. Such furrowed faces are not uncommon in Nepal, where the harsh weather of both winter and summer takes its toll over the years. The Inuit have a similar practice: their masks are carved from whalebone but they're also intended to dispel spiteful spirits.

<
Mask from the Himalayas made from a mushroom to frighten away evil spirits.

BON APPÉTIT

This item of exotica would certainly have been a conversation piece. It's an *iCula ni bokola,* literally translated; a cannibal fork, with which to eat human flesh. Carved entirely from wood, it comes from the Fiji islands, where it would have belonged to an important member of a cannibal tribe. Such high-ranking individuals were considered too hallowed to touch anything unsanctified, such as food, so they would be fed by an attendant using a fork like this.

A cannibal fork from the Fiji islands: a curiosity from the collection of Theatrum Mundi in Arezzo.

Javanese villages were all the rage at the world fairs of the late nineteenth century.

JAVANESE SENSATION

The summer of 1883 saw the first-ever world fair to be held in the Netherlands. A group of Javanese and Sumatrans was brought to Amsterdam especially for the occasion. They were a regular anthropological sensation as they apparently went about their usual daily occupations in a reconstructed and railed-off Indonesian village. But reactions to the Javanese village were mixed. It certainly garnered plenty of oohs and aahs, but on the other hand it was noted that 'The "villagers" were badly educated, badly dressed, badly paid and, into the bargain, brutalized and reviled if they complained.' In 1892 a troupe of Egyptians complete with camels descended on Amsterdam. Their reception was lukewarm. 'What we are shown is – if I may say so – a zoo put together from such dregs as can be tempted by a few pieces of silver to make a tour of the chief cities of Europe.'

>

The *Museum Wormianum* installation, a recreation of and commentary on Ole Worm's *Wunderkammer*, by American contemporary artist and photographer Rosamond Purcell.

METAL
COCHLEÆ

LICA
METALLIA
MINERALIA
URBINATA
CONCHILIA
MARIANA
UM PARTES
CONCHILIATA
SALIA
SEMINA
TERRÆ
RADICES

Chapter 5

TERRA INCOGNITA

Imaginary Exotica

—

There's plenty of wonder
left in the universe,
even after we have examined all
the clues nature has thrown our way.
I really believe that our imaginations
have not even begun to exhaust
the possibilities of existence.

Lawrence M. Krauss (1954)

—

<

Contemporary artist Daniel Horowitz paints absurd scenes from a fictive safari.

Exotica are not merely eye candy. They're also implicit evidence of the way in which European collectors viewed the world. That is why collections of exotica are interesting on more than one level. Not only are they assemblages of objects from distant lands and cultures, they're also a way of bringing curiosity and dominance together under one flag, as it were. The *Wunderkammer* displays a dualistic worldview: us against them – western civilization versus exotic cultures. Geographical origin was sometimes a side issue; it really didn't matter whether an object came from Africa, America or Oceania. An item might be conveniently said to be from the 'Indies', but it might really come from Japan or Africa. Exotic objects were ripped from their original context to enhance the self-image of Europe in much the same way that 'wild' animals were slaughtered in the Colosseum in Rome to emphasize to the amused audience the hegemony of the Roman Empire. There was nothing accidental about the placing of Jerusalem at the centre of a medieval map and the banishing to the edges of all manner of bizarre creatures and peoples. Whether they existed or not was beside the point; the centre was the norm, the edge was the territory of the abnormal. Those unknown beasts and beings that were figuratively falling off the map are fascinating, because in them you see man's imagination (and therefore his fears) reflected. Things that are dangerous and unknown are also fascinating and potentially enriching. 'Foreign' influences destabilized the world order, but at the same time they opened up new possibilities – for trade and territorial expansion on the one hand, for wild legends on the other. Or for a combination of the two: a market for mythical collectibles from that terra incognita.

The wish lists of the earliest collectors were determined by what was contained in natural histories and travelogues – by the animals, shells, objects and marvellous beings that they described. Even if the information in the book was false or wrong, it still created a demand for certain objects or creatures. The horn of a unicorn, for example, or the claws of a griffin – items from animals that were only known from texts or prints. It follows that collecting was initially an occupation for the literary and intellectual elite. If you couldn't read, you couldn't build a collection. But even if you knew everything the books had to tell, you were still being led up the garden path. Fabulous beasts and fraudulent fakes masquerading as exotica were everywhere. Such monsters were good business for centuries.

Clover leaf map of 1581, with Jerusalem as the centre of the world.

MEDICINAL MALARKEY

The extraordinary thing is that many exotic animals or plants were believed to have medicinal properties – among them agate, beryl, coral, powdered rhinoceros or unicorn horn, and even snake tongues (in reality fossilized sharks' teeth) or a flayed lion skin. All of these were naturalia not to be found exactly on the doorstep, or that, like the unicorn horn, simply didn't exist at all. According to the medieval cleric Gerald of Wales (1146–1223), the reasoning behind that strange origin was simple: whence much evil comes, there must be many remedies against those evil powers too.

—

ANONYMOUS DRAGON

The trouble with many books about exotic fauna and flora was that their authors, be they scholars or explorers, had not seen many of the creatures they wrote about. They relied on other people's supposedly eyewitness accounts or on earlier written sources, or simply dreamt something up. Take the French naturalist Pierre Belon (1517–1564), for instance. In his *L'histoire naturelle des estranges poissons marins* (*The Natural History of Foreign Sea Fish*), published in 1551, he describes rays that jump out of the water to catch fish. Where he got his information is a mystery, and he couldn't possibly have seen that technique in nature. The writers and researchers of the time had few qualms about blending fantasy and reality. Even the most well-intentioned scholars, such as the Amsterdam apothecary Albertus Seba (1665–1736), occasionally fell into that trap. Seba invested in his own illustrator in order to record his huge collection of naturalia and exotica. Yet his catalogue also includes a seven-headed dragon. That picture was calmly 'borrowed' from an older catalogue of another collector's cabinet of curiosities, and that other collector had in turn either invented it or pirated it from yet another source.

—

UNICORN HYPE

Narwhal tusks are among the most sought-after exotica. It was long believed that such a tusk was an alicorn, the horn of the unicorn, a mythological horse-like creature with a long, slender and incredibly sharp horn projecting from its forehead. The horn was rare and many magical properties were attributed to it. That is why one end of the alicorn in the Abbey of Saint-Denis – famed for its astonishing Treasury – rested in water. A dose of *eau do licorne*, as the healing water was called, could be obtained on request. St Paul's Cathedral and Westminster Abbey in London both had an alicorn, as did the Basilica of San Marco in Venice. Rather than lying in water, the third of those horns was partially scraped and the powder was used as medicine. According to the German Benedictine mystic Hildegard of Bingen (1098–1179), it was not only the horn itself that possessed curative powers: the entire animal was therapeutic. Beneath its horn was a piece

In 1694 Pierre Pomet summarized the 'existing' types of unicorn.

of transparent metal in which you saw your face reflected. She also noted a recipe for an ointment made from egg yolk and powdered unicorn liver, said to be particularly beneficial to leprosy sufferers. No self-respecting Renaissance ruler could be without an alicorn. At the height of their desirability a unicorn horn was worth ten times its weight in gold, to the extreme that in 1660 the German scholar Johann Frederick Hubrick wondered rhetorically, 'Is there any prince, duke or king in the world who has not either seen or possessed, and regarded as among the most precious of his possessions, a unicorn's horn?'

>

Olaus Magnus's 1539 *Carta Marina*, the earliest known map of the Nordic lands, complete with details and place names.

ISLANDIA
MARE GLACIALE
FARE
TILE
BALENA
ORCA
ORCADES XXXIII
HETLANDIA
NORVEGIA
NORMORIA
TILEMARCHIA
MARE DEUCALIDONICUM
SCOTIAE PARS
ANGLIAE PARS
OCCIANUS BRITANNICUS
MARE GERMANICUM
DANIA
HOLSATIA
FRISIA ORIENTALIS
FRISIA OCCIDENTALIS
GEOGRAPHIAE STVDIOSO TYPOGRAPHVS.

FINMARCHIA
SCRICFINNIA
BIARMIA
LACVS ALBVS
LAPPIA OCCIDENTALIS
LAPPIA ORIENTALIS
MARE BOTNICV
BOTNIA OCCIDENTALIS
BOTNIA Orientalis
CARELIA
ANGERMANNIA
MEDELPADIA
MARE SVETICVM
FINLANDIA
MAREFINONICVM
MOSCOVIE PARS
GESTRICIA
VPLANDIA
RODIN
RVSSIA ALBA
NOGARDIA
OLAVS GOTH BENIGNO LECTORI
MARE LIVONICVM
ESTHIA
LIVONIA AVSTRALIS
RVSSIA
GOTLANDIA
CVRETES
MARE GOTHICVM
SAMOGETHIA
LITVANIE PARS

SHARP PRACTICE

At some point the unicorn fable had to be laid to rest. Apart from anything else, the whale hunters of the far north knew perfectly well where the purported alicorns came from. That didn't stop them from selling them, via intermediaries, to dealers with connections to exotica collectors. In 1555 the Swedish diplomat and scholar Olaus Magnus (1490–1557) described the narwhal as 'a sea monster with a very long horn on its forehead that can drill through ships and men'. Whalers hunting in the waters around Greenland regarded them as 'the unicorns of the sea', and their 'horns' were sold as magical objects. This went on until the Danish naturalist and collector Ole Worm (1588–1654; see also Chapter 1) debunked the myth once and for all. In 1638 he made the first reference to the real origin of the 'horn' in his *Medicarum Institutionum Libri*. It was, he said, a horn from the jaw of the male narwhal. A little less than a century later, in 1714, writing in his *Museum museorum*, the German collector Michael Bernhard Valentini (1657–1729) also declared that the unicorn was a 'total fiction'. Nevertheless, people continued to believe in the therapeutic properties of the unicorn until well into the eighteenth century. Even though the myth has been exploded, narwhal tusks still turn up at auction. They continue to be a collectible item of exotica, for not only do they have great decorative value, they come with the added advantage of a fascinating magical story as well. What's more, new chapters are still being written, for scientific research now shows that the narwhal's tusk is not so much a weapon as an ultra-sensitive sensory organ that helps narwhals perceive the environment around them. The legend continues ...

—

EYE TO EYE

Elephant skulls were long believed to be the skulls of cyclops, the monstrous race with a single eye in the centre of their forehead. And it doesn't take much imagination to see why, for indeed the central nasal cavity where the elephant's trunk was attached would be just the right size for a cyclopean eye. If you'd never seen a real elephant there was no reason to disbelieve the existence of the cyclops. Look through the eyes of collectors from the Middle Ages to the Renaissance and Baroque and it's not hard to understand why people also saw coconuts as something fabulous. No European tree produced such large nuts or seeds, so the coconut obviously had to have come from a mythical, divine plant. In Renaissance *Wunderkammern*, it was sometimes called the 'Indian nut' as it arrived in Europe via the ports of the subcontinent. Due to its strange hard shape, magical properties were ascribed to it. For instance, if the wine in a drinking cup made from a coconut was poisoned, the coconut itself was said to act as an antidote. The nut was immensely popular with collectors – and with goldsmiths, who were often tasked with creating an exquisite mount for it. Thus the coconut was elevated into a work of art created by nature but confined in a form devised by man. The endless contest between the human and the divine was typical of cabinets of curiosity.

When the first duck-billed platypus skin arrived in London, everyone was convinced that such an improbable animal must be a fake.

A DUCK-BILLED WHAT?

Mythology and the market for fabulous beasts could sometimes be quite a hindrance to science. Take the case of the duck-billed platypus, for example. It was a long time before scientists could bring themselves to believe there was any such thing. When British colonists first encountered the curious creature native to Tasmania and Australia in 1788, they prepared a preserved specimen, ready for zoological research. But when the skin arrived in London in 1789, biologists and zoologists greeted it with extreme scepticism. They thought it was yet another dragon hoax, like all the others that were going the rounds. There was a developing market for mounted hybrids – exotic creatures assembled from parts of different animals. Thus 'new' species were created that were 'rare' by definition and therefore very desirable. As for the much-maligned duck-billed platypus, its existence was finally established by the English botanist and zoologist George Shaw (1751–1813), who carried out extensive research and published his results in *The Naturalist's Miscellany*. If you happen to be in the neighbourhood of the Natural History Museum in London, you can see that legendary specimen – it's still there.

I chose life over death
for myself and my friends.
I believe it is in our nature to explore,
to reach out into the unknown.
The only true failure would be
not to explore at all.

Ernest Shackleton (1874–1922), British polar explorer

<

Skull by Belgian contemporary artist Jan Fabre
(2010 - mixture of wing cases of the scarab, polymers, stuffed bird).

Dragon-like creatures preserved in alcohol, from the collection of The World of Kina (Ghent).

HYBRID CLAW

From the Middle Ages onward, even the most modest collection of exotica had to include a griffin claw. No one had ever seen a griffin in the flesh, but the claws were highly desirable (in reality, the 'claws' were usually buffalo horns). The fact that the claws 'existed' confirmed the existence of griffins. The mythological creature occurs in the works of writers such as the brothers Grimm, Goethe and Flaubert, and of course in J. K. Rowling's Harry Potter series – where griffin claw is one of the ingredients of Strengthening Solution – and in the World of Warcraft computer game. But the earliest traces of it date back as far as the fifteenth century BCE: images of griffins couchant flank the throne in the palace of Knossos in Crete. The Venetian explorer Marco Polo (1254–1324) described them in his travel diaries. They lived, so he was told, on islands to the south of Madagascar: 'But you must know that they are by no means such as men in our country suppose, or as we portray them – half-bird and half-lion. According to the report of those who have seen them ... in build they are just like eagles but of the most colossal size ... so huge and bulky that one of them can pounce on an elephant and carry it up to a great height in the air. Then it lets go, so that the elephant drops to earth and is smashed to pulp, whereupon the gryphon bird perches on the carcase and feeds at its ease. They add that they have a wing span of thirty paces and that their wing feathers are twelve paces long and of a thickness proportionate to their length.' The German Dominican Albertus Magnus (1200–1280) also included a passage on griffins in *De Animalibus*: 'According to folk tales, griffins are said to be birds, but their credibility as real animals is not based on the experience of philosophers nor the evidence of natural science. The tales relate how the foreparts of these birds – i.e. their head, beak, wings and fore feet – resemble an eagle, though on a much larger scale. The posterior portion of the animal, including the tail and rear legs, looks like a lion. The fore feet have long aquiline talons, while the rear feet have short but massive leonine claws which they use as cups for drinking; thus griffins are said to have both long and short claws. They are supposed to live in the mountains of the extreme north, are especially inimical to horses and men, and are so strong they can carry off a horse and its rider. Their mountain eyries are claimed to be laden with gold and gems, particularly emeralds. The stories also tell that griffins deposit agates in their nests because of the agate's special beneficial properties.'

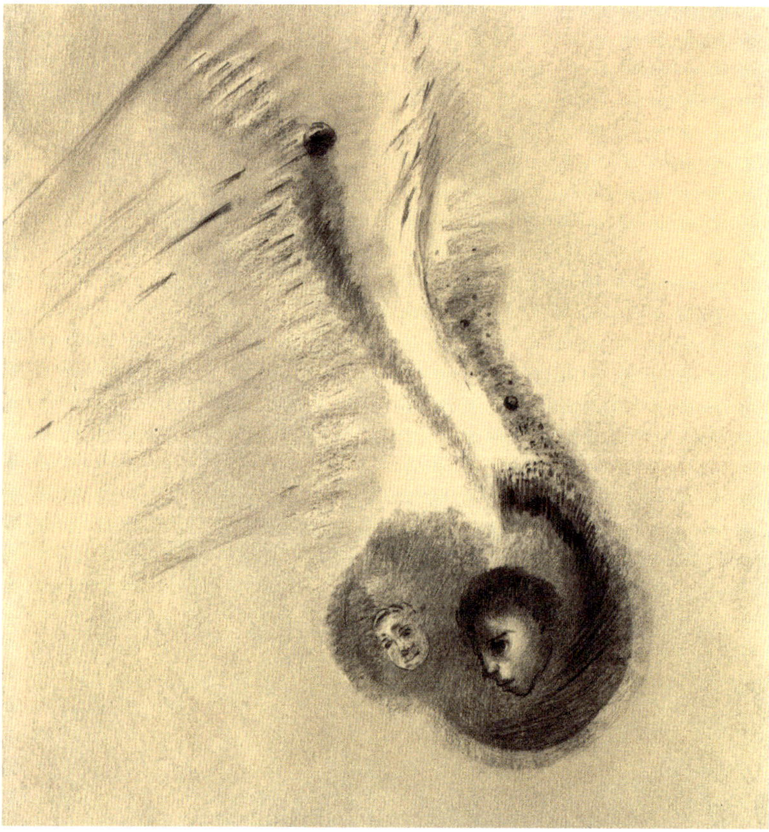

The artist Odilon Redon based many of his works on mythological beings, such as the sciapods, creatures with one giant foot.

A DOG'S LIFE

One particularly strange race was the cynocephali, who sported a dog's head on a human body. They were without doubt one of the most discussed exotic races in the 'fantasy' category. Like those of the griffin, descriptions and illustrations of them varied enormously. Some writers depicted the dog men as urbane citizens in European clothing, while others were convinced that they were no better than cannibals who preferred their strangers raw and highly spiced. Marco Polo was at least honest, admitting that he had not actually seen the cynocephali – though only because he had not travelled far enough. But the fact that he had seen other marvellous animals, such as elephants and rhinoceroses, made it almost certain that he'd missed the cynocephali purely by mischance. Even the Italian author Umberto Eco (1932–2016) writes about the cynocephali in *Baudolino,* a picaresque novel published in 2000 and set in the twelfth century. *Baudolino* also features sciapods: a mythological human-like race with a single huge foot. Eco's book takes place on the border between mythological fiction and historical reality, the very territory to which collections of exotica belong.

Giraffa polyzoaria turriformis, a fictitious animal scene by Daniel Horowitz.

Simia Paniscus Linn.

Altenwanger del. *Tyroff sc.*

*Man is merely a common product,
the monster an uncommon product.
Both equally natural,
equally necessary, equally part of this
universal and general order of things.
And what is astonishing about this?
All creatures intermingle
with each other, consequently with
all species. Every animal is more or less
man, every mineral is more or
less plant, every plant more or
less animal. There is nothing precise
in nature.*

Denis Diderot (1713–1784), philosopher

<

The *Simia araneaformis*, a contemporary fabulous beast, by Daniel Horowitz.

HYBRID CREATURES

Man–animal composites provided a recurrent theme in medieval literature. That kind of hybrid life form dominated many an author's imagination. They not only wrote about sciapods and cynocephali but also about the psilli, who emit a poison that is deadly to snakes, and the onocentaur, a creature half-man, half-ass. In 1575 Cornelius Gemma (1535–1578), professor of medicine at Leuven's university, drew up a list of all the monstrous races he knew of. In *De naturae divinis characterismis* he refers to 'men completely wild in appearance and way of life', amongst whom he includes 'fauns, satyrs, androgynes, ichthyophages, sciapods, hippopodes, anthropophagi, pygmies' and so forth. 'Moreover', he added, 'it is not necessary to go to the New World to find beings of this sort'.

—

DRAGONOLOGY

The Bologna-born Ulisse Aldrovandi (1522–1605) was not only an influential naturalist and collector of naturalia and exotica; he was also the go-to person for anything to do with dragons. How do you acquire such a reputation? By having a pickled dragon in your private collection and making no secret about it. And, of course, by studying dragons. When Gregory XIII received the papal tiara in 1572, a terrifying dragon appeared in the hills around Bologna, or so the story goes. Aldrovandi – then professor of natural sciences at Bologna university – was rushed to the scene to inspect the carcass of the fearful beast. He came to a somewhat surprising conclusion: the fabulous creature was a good omen for Gregory's papal appointment. And with that he made himself immortal. But Aldrovandi went one step further: he produced a seven-volume book recording everything he knew about all sorts of dragons. The encyclopedic *Monstrorum Historia* first appeared in 1642, almost four decades after Aldrovandi's death. It reads as an eccentric collection of deformed, hybrid 'manimals'. Aldrovandi insisted that the woodcuts illustrating the book were based on 'real' monsters, though perhaps we can be forgiven for doubting that.

<

Thomas Grünfeld's *Misfits*: impossible blends of different animals

The fake mermaid of the British Museum.
Right: H.L. Stephens cartoon of P.T. Barnum, 1851.

FIJI FAKES

Mermaids are not just fabulous creatures found only in fairy tales. They really did exist, at least if we're to believe in the stuffed specimens in the collections of the British Museum in London, the Muséum national d'Histoire naturelle in Paris and the Museum voor Volkskunde in Leiden. All three museums have a counterfeit sea monster of this sort: a piece of prepared illusion, covered in fish scales. Many of the mermaids that arrived in Europe came by way of the Dutchman Jan Cock Blomhoff (1779–1853), director of the Dutch trading post on Dejima island in the harbour of Nagasaki in Japan. The most celebrated specimen is, of course, the famous 'Feejee Mermaid' displayed by Phineas Taylor (P. T.) Barnum (1810–1891), American master showman and entrepreneur, in 1846. His hybrid creature – very skilfully made from a monkey's head and a fish's body – attracted full houses of voyeuristic spectators. No doubt the sensation-seeking audience was also drawn in by Barnum's canny advertising campaign – the picture of the mermaid in the newspapers showed a beautiful creature with flowing tresses and naked breasts. The hype was very effective, as was the buzz that surrounded his travelling menagerie. Billed as 'The Greatest Show on Earth', it featured exotic people, dwarves, elephants and 'Indians', just like Carl Hagenbeck's *Völkerschauen* (see Chapter 3).

P. T. Barnum

HUM - BUG.

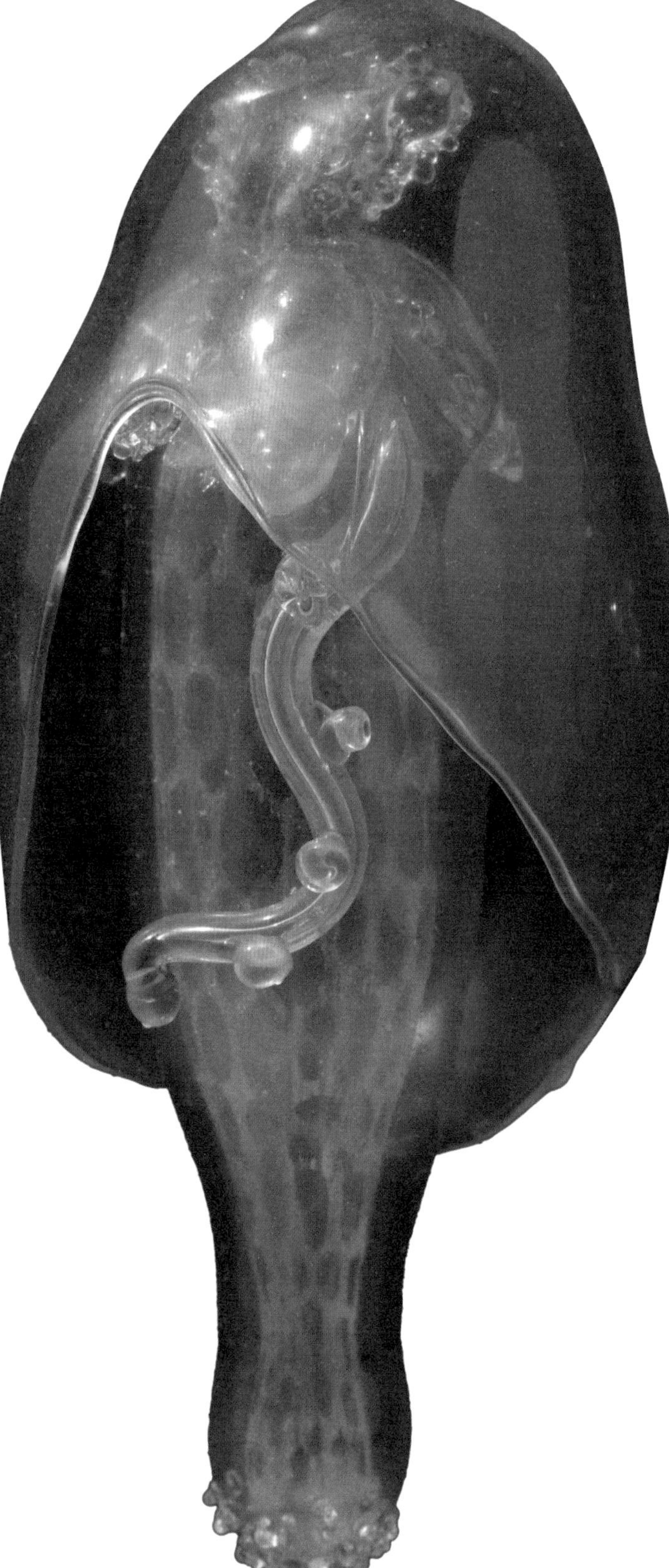

GLASSY EYED

Between 1863 and 1890 Leopold and Rudolf Blaschka, a father-and-son team of glass-blowers from Dresden, dumbfounded friends and enemies alike with their incredible glass sea creatures. From octopuses to anemones, jellyfish to starfish, the Blaschkas reproduced them in glass with extraordinary accuracy. They were not intended as works of art but as educational material for students of marine fauna. Only invertebrates were replicated because glass was the best medium for imitating their translucent structure. In 1853 Leopold, a Czech goldsmith and gem-cutter, had lost both his wife and father, who died within a short time of each other. Distraught and in need of distraction, he travelled to America. During the ocean crossing he would spend the nights watching, with a sense of wonder, the luminescent creatures that dwelled in the ocean, and he began to think about making them in glass. As soon as he was back in his workshop, he first tried to create orchids and then marine creatures in blown glass. As his son would do later, he based his creations on specimens preserved in alcohol or zoological drawings by the likes of German zoologist Ernst Haeckel. Later, the Blaschkas installed their own saltwater aquarium in which they could observe living marine animals. There is a beguiling poetry about their work, which is as fascinating in its way as Else Bostelmann's paintings of deep sea creatures (see Chapter 2).

—

GLASS WONDER

Without doubt the Blaschkas' work inspired contemporary Danish glass artist Steffen Dam. His objects look extraordinarily like specimens of marine creatures such as jellyfish or anemones preserved in alcohol. In reality, they're fantasies, marvels of glass-blowing, incredibly delicate works that defy the imagination. His glass specimens are an ode to the variety of the animal kingdom. His creativity doesn't stop there, though. Dam has no desire to capture or record nature as collectors of exotica do. What does fill his glass is unpredictable poetry – reason enough to include it in a contemporary *Wunderkammer.*

<

Item out of the Blaschka collection of the University Museum Utrecht.

>

Specimen Jars, 2013. Danish artist Steffen Dams 'jellyfish' are made of glass.

ANIMAL REMODELLER

American contemporary artist Daniel Horowitz also sets out for terra incognita in his work, subversively reappropriating original eighteenth- and nineteenth-century engravings and lithographs like a forger of history. He retells the tale of a fictive safari expedition, including fantastical beasts and heroic encounters between man and animal. He adds a layer of surrealism to the authentic animal prints (which as a rule are not terribly realistic anyway) that were popular in the eighteenth and nineteenth centuries. Horowitz is at his best when he invents new species or when he places existing animals in bizarre contexts. Two elephants share a common trunk, which doesn't make drinking any easier. A flamingo's disproportionately long neck has snaked so far that its head is quite out of the picture. In a twist of creation a monkey suddenly has four arms but no head. Horowitz's work comments on man's passion for discovery, which has led to the extinction or overhunting of so many animal species. He also shows how our perception of hunting has changed over time. But above all, he shows how man has dealt with animals over the centuries. 'I hope that for a split second my works are seen as authentic, with the result that the spectator must very consciously ask himself what he sees,' Horowitz says. 'That's why I also give the animals Latin names that sound very realistic. I put people on the wrong foot. And my guiding principle in doing that is humour: an essential tool for exposing dark subjects.'

> & >>

Phoenicopterus longicollis and *Simia geminoidea*, contemporary fabulous beasts by Daniel Horowitz.

FLAMINGOES.

HEAVENS!

They're a little less common than minerals or shells, but meteorites certainly belong to the realm of exotica. And – like the unicorn horn and the *coco de mer* – for a long time there was confusion about where the 'heaven stones' came from. In 1576 the Spanish governor of a province in northern Argentina ordered an investigation into the type of metal the indigenous people used to make their extraordinarily strong weapons. The metal, it was said, had fallen from the sky at a place whose name the Spanish translated as Campo del Cielo (Field of Heaven). And indeed, a large mass of pure metal was found there, but the place was assumed to be an iron mine. Not until 1783, when samples of the metal were examined by the Royal Society in London, was it established that the 'heaven stones' were more than ten million years old.

—

TWENTY-FIRST-CENTURY EXOTICA

A thought to end with ... Does collecting exotica still make sense? Which items of exotica belong in a contemporary *Wunderkammer*? To put it another way, in this twenty-first century is there anything that can still be called exotic in a world that has become so small, in which there is no longer any terra incognita? What are today's collectible marvels? What could a collector still long for, now that every part of the globe has been discovered and exploited? These are questions posed by the Italian antiquarians behind Theatrum Mundi, who build what they call 'twenty-first-century cabinets of curiosity'. Of course, there are still narwhal tusks, stuffed tropical birds and indigenous ornaments – classic exotica that are essential as historical references to the traditional 'chambers of wonder'. But these antiquarians also add dinosaur bones. And – very special items – used Russian and American space suits. Why?

The universe and the cosmos have fascinated scholars for centuries. And science fiction writers such as Jules Verne and H. G. Wells created fantastic tales about space that have captivated generations of readers. Thanks to the space programmes the United States and Russia have followed since the second half of the twentieth century, the most exotic destination that still remains – space – is now also within the traveller's reach. Souvenirs of those expeditions have the same emotional value as the shells or tropical birds brought back five hundred years ago from journeys to undiscovered lands. To quote American naturalist and dinosaur expert Roy Chapman Andrews (1884–1960): 'Today there remain but a few small areas of the world's map unmarked by explorers' trails. Human courage and endurance have conquered the Poles; the secrets of the tropical jungles have been revealed. The highest mountains on earth have heard the voice of man. But this doesn't mean that the youth of the future has no new world to vanquish. It means that the explorer must change his methods.'

Illustration from *20,000 Leagues Under the Sea* by Jules Verne (1828-1905), engraved by Henri Theophile Hildibrand (1824-97).

SELECT LIST OF SOURCES

ALDROVANDI, ULISSE, *Monstrorum Historia*, 1642.

ALDROVANDI, ULISSE, *Ornithologiae*, 1599.

ALLEN, DAVID ELLISTON, *The Naturalist in Britain: A Social History*, Princeton University Press, 1976.

ANDREWS, ROY CHAPMAN, *On the Trail of Ancient Man*, G.P. Putnam's Sons, 1926.

AUDUBON, JOHN JAMES, *The Birds of America: from original drawings by John James Audubon*, 1827-1838.

BALLINTIJN, G., *Rumphius. De blinde ziener van Ambon*, Uitgeversmaatschappij W. de Haan, 1944.

BATES, HENRY WALTER, *The Naturalist on the River Amazons*, London 1864.

BARBER, RICHARD & RICHES, ANNE, *A Dictionary of Fabulous Beasts*, MacMillan, 1971.

BEEBE, WILLIAM, *Half Mile Down*, New York Zoological Society, 1935.

BELON, PIERRE, *L'histoire naturelle des estranges poissons marins*, Regnaud Chaudiere, 1551.

BROWN, ANDREW & GRAEME SMALL, Court and Civic Society in the Burgundian Low Countries, c.1420-1530, Manchester University Press, 2007.

CAILLOIS, ROGER, *La lecture des pierres*, Editions Xavier Barral, 2014.

CHEMEL, FRANÇOIS, *François Sommer, un temps d'avance*, Buchet/Chastel, 2013.

CHENU, JEAN-CHARLES, *Illustrations conchyliologiques ou description et figures de toutes les coquilles connues vivantes et fossiles, classées suivant le système de Lamarck modifié d'après les progrès de la science et comprenant les genres nouveaux et les espèces récemment découvertes*, 1842.

CIARLO, DAVID, *Advertising Empire: Race and Visual Culture in Imperial Germany*, Harvard University Press, 2011.

CIOBANU, ESTELLA ANTOANETA, *The Spectacle of the Body in Late Medieval England*, Lumen, 2012.

DASTON, LORRAINE en PARK, KATHARINE, *Wonders and the Order of Nature, 1150-1750*, Zone Books, 1998.

DAVIS, NATALIE ZEMON, '"Leo Africanus" Presents Africa to Europeans' in Joaneth Spicer (ed.), *Revealing the African presence in Renaissance Europe*. Walters Art Museum, 2012.

DE LÉRY, JEAN, *History to a Voyage to the Land of Brazil*, 1578.

DE VITRY, JACQUES, *Historia Orientalis*, 1216-1227.

DEMEULEMEESTER, THIJS en LEMAITRE, JEROEN, *Wonders are Collectible. Taxidermie: verstilde schoonheid*, Lannoo, 2016.

DÉZALLIER D'ARGENVILLE, ANTOINE-JOSEPH, *La conchyliologie, ou Histoire naturelle des coquilles de mer, d'eau douce, terrestres et fossils*, Guillaume de Bure, Parijs, 1780.

EDGINTON, BRIAN & WATERTON, CHARLES, *A Biography*, The Lutterworth Press, 1996.

FINDLEN, PAULA, *Possessing Nature: Museums, Collecting and Scientific Culture in Early Modern Italy*, University of California Press, 1996.

FRIEDMAN, JOHN BLOCK, *The Monstrous Races in Medieval Art and Thought*, Syracuse University Press, 2000.

GAMMA, CORNELIUS, *De naturae divinis characterismis*, 1575.

GOULD, JOHN, *A Century of Birds from the Himalaya Mountains*, 1831.

GOULD, JOHN, *Exotische Vögel*, RGA-Verlag, 1991.

GRICE, GORDON, *Cabinet of Curiosities, Collecting and Understanding the Wonders of the Natural World*, Workman Publishing Company, 2015.

HERBERT, KARI en LEWIS-JONES, HUW, *Het logboek van de ontdekkingsreiziger*, Omniboek, 2016.

HOLMES, RACHEL, *The Hottentot Venus: The Life and Death of Saartjie Baartman: Born 1789 - buried 2002*, Bloomsbury Publishing, 2007.

IMPERATO, FERRANTE, *Dell'historia naturale di Ferrante Imperato Napolitano libri XX VIII*, Napels, Constantia Vitale, 1599.

JANCEY, MERYL, *Mappa Mundi. The Map of the World in Hereford Cathedral*, Hereford Cathedral Enterprises, 1994.

KAREN, WONDERS, *Habitat Diorama's: Illusions of Wilderness in Museums of Natural History*, Almqvist & Wiksell, 1993.

KIRCHER, ATHANASIUS, *Musurgia Universalis*, 1650.

MANCALL, PETER C. (ED), *Travel Narratives from the Age of Discovery: An Anthology*, Oxford University Press, 2006.

MANDEVILLE, JOHN, *The Book of Marvels and Travels (trans. Anthony Bale)*, Oxford University Press, 2012.

MARR, ALEXANDER, *Curiosity and Wonder from the Renaissance to the Enlightenment*, Ashgate Publishing, 2006.

MCFALL, MATTHEW, *The Little Book of Awe and Wonder: A Cabinet of Curiosities*, Independent Thinking Press, 2013.

MULDER, HANS en ZEVENHUIZEN, ERIK (red.), *De natuur op papier*, Artis Bibliotheek, 2013.

NEICKEL, CASPER F., *Museographia*, 1727.

OGILVIE, BRIAN W., *The Science of Describing: Natural History in Renaissance Europe*, The University of Chicago Press, 2008.

Paré, Ambroise, *Des monstres et prodiges, 1573*, ed. Jean Céard, Librairie Droz, Genève, 1971.

Pearce, Susan M., *On Collecting: An investigation into Collecting in the European Tradition*, Routledge, Londen, 1995.

Platt, Peter G., *Wonders, Marvels and Monsters in Early Modern Culture*, University of Delaware Press, 2000.

Poliquin, Rachel, *The Breathless Zoo, Taxidermy and the Cultures of Longing*, The Pennsylvania State University Press, 2012.

Polo, Marco, *The Travels of Marco Polo, (trans. Ronald Latham, 1958)*, Penguin Books, 1986.

Price, David (red.), *The Travels of Sir John Mandeville*, Macmillan and Co., 1900.

Quicchelberg, Samuel, *Inscriptiones vel tituli theatri amplissimi, complectentis rerum universitatis singulas materias et imagines eximias*, Adam Berg, München, 1565.

Ritvo, Harriet, *The Platypus and the Mermaid, and Other Figments of the Classifying Imagination*, Harvard University Press, 1997.

Rothfels, Nigel, *Savages and Beasts: The Birth of the Modern Zoo*, The John Hopkins University Press, 2002.

Rudolph, Conrad (ed.), *A Companion to Medieval Art: Romanesque and Gothic in Northern Europe: Romanesque and Gothic in Northern Europe*, Blackwell Publishing Ltd. Chichester, 2010.

Scheuchzer, Johann Jakob, *Kupfer-Bibel (Physica Sacra)*, 1731-1735.

Seba, Albertus, *Cabinet of Natural Curiosities*, Taschen, 2015.

Shepard, Odell, *The Lore of the Unicorn*, n.p. 1930.

Simpson, Patrick Allegaert, *De exotische mens. Andere culturen als amusement*, Lannoo, 2009. Sleigh, Charlotte, *The Paper Zoo. 500 years of animals in Art*, The British Library, 2016.

Smith, Pamela H. & Findlen, Paula (eds), Merchants and Marvels. Commerce, *Science and Art in Early Modern Europe*, Routledge, 2002.

Staden, Hans, *Hans Staden's True History: An Account of Cannibal Captivity in Brazil (ed. & trans. Niel L. Whitehead & Michael Harbsmeier)*, Duke University Press, 2008.

Staden, Hans, *Warhaftige Historia und beschreibung eyner Landtschafft der Wilden Nacketen, Grimmigen Menschfresser-Leuthen in der Newenwelt America gelegen (True Story and Description of a Country of Wild, Naked, Grim, Man-eating People in the New World, America)*, 1557.

Lord Stanley of Alderley, *The First Voyage Round the World by Magellan. Translated From the Accounts of Pigafetta and Other Contemporary Writers. Accompanied by Original Documents, with Notes and an Introduction*, The Hakluyt Society, 1874.

Stepan Leys, Nancy, *Picturing Tropical Nature*, Cornell University, Ithaca, 2001.

Tree, Isabella, *The Ruling Passion of John Gould: A Biography of the Bird Man*, Barrie and Jenkins, Londen, 1991.

Trentmann, Frank (ed.), *The Oxford Handbook of the History of Consumption*, Oxford University Press Inc., 2012.

Turner, Alexis, *Taxidermy*, Thames & Hudson, 2013.

Valentini, Michael Bernhard, *Museum Museorum*, 1704-1714.

Van Tilbury, Gervasius, *Otia Imperialia*, 1210.

Vaughan, Richard, *Philip the Good*, The Boydel Press, (1970) 2004.

Wallace, Alfred Russel, *A Narrative Of Travels on The Amazon and Rio Negro, with an Account of The Native Tribes, and Observations on the Climate, Geology, and Natural History of The Amazon Valley*, Ward, Lock and Co., 1890.

Wallace, Alfred Russel, *My Life. A Record of Events and Opinions*, Chapman & Hall, Ltd., 1905.

Waterton, Charles, *Wanderings in South America*, B. Fellowes, Londen, 1828.

Wexler, Philip (ed.), *Toxicology in the Middle Ages and Renaissance*, Academic Press (Elsevier), 2017.

Worm, Ole, *Museum Wormianum, seu, Historia rerum rariorum: tam naturalium, quam artificialium, tam domesticarum, quam exoticarum, quae Hafniae Danorum in aedibus authoris servantur*, 1655.

X, *All my possessions for a moment of time, catalogue 14*, Finch & Co, 2009.

X, *Animals in Brazil: Frans Post*, Rijksmuseum Amsterdam, 2016.

X, *Exotica*, Kunstkammer Georg Laue München, 2012.

X, *Filtered through Time, catalogue 19*, Finch & Co, 2012.

X, *Genius & Art, catalogue 25*, Finch & Co, 2015.

X, *Great things and full of wonder I shall unfold, catalogue 16*, Finch & Co, 2010.

X, *Half as old as Time, catalogue 17*, Finch & Co, 2011.

X, *Het Gulden Cabinet, Koninklijk Museum bij Rockox te gast*, Bezoekersgids, 2015.

X, *Kostbare Bestecke*, Kunstkammer Georg Laue, München, 2012.

X, *Liber monstrorum de diversis generibus*, ed. Corrado Bologna, Bompiani, Milaan, 1977.

X, *Miracles, Marvels and Monsters, catalogue 12*, Finch & Co, 2008.

X, *Passion, Possessions & Power, catalogue 22*, Finch & Co, 2014.

X, *Rituals & Relics, catalogue 27*, Finch & Co, 2016.

X, *The XXI Century Cabinet of Curiosities*, Theatrum Mundi Arezzo, 2016.

X, *Veilingcatalogus taxidermie*, Rob Michiels Auctions, november 2016.

X, *Vente Chambre des merveilles III*, Millon & Associés Belgique, 2017.

PHOTO CREDITS

p. 2 University of Glasgow Library, Special Collections; pp. 4-5 Rijksmuseum, Amsterdam; p. 6 Courtesy of Oskar Proctor & The Viktor Wynd Museum of Curiosities; p. 8 Natural History Museum, London, UK / Bridgeman Images; p. 9 Rijksmuseum, Amsterdam; p. 10 Science & Society Picture Library / Getty Images; p. 13 ART Collection / Alamy Stock Photo; p. 14 Deutsches Museum; p. 16 RMN – Grand Palais (Musée du Louvre) / Gérard Blot; p. 19 The Dean and Chapter of Hereford Cathedral and the Hereford Mappa Mundi Trust; pp. 20 – 21 Rijksmuseum, Amsterdam; p. 23 Auction House Millon, Brussels; p. 24 Courtesy of Darwin, Sinke & van Tongeren; p. 26 INTERFOTO / Alamy Stock Photo; p. 28 Deutsches Museum; p. 31 Courtesy of Skoklosters Slott Museum / photo by Samuel Uhrdin; pp. 32 – 33 Private Collection / Bridgeman Images; pp. 34 – 35 Santiago Caruso; p. 37 Rijksmuseum, Amsterdam; p. 38 RMN – Grand Palais (Musée du Louvre) / Gérard Blot; p. 41 The George Peabody Library, The Sheridan Libraries, John Hopkins University; p. 42 Rijksmuseum, Amsterdam; p. 43 Rijksmuseum, Amsterdam; p. 45 The George Peabody Library, The Sheridan Libraries, John Hopkins University; p. 46 Rijksmuseum, Amsterdam; pp. 48 – 49 The George Peabody Library, The Sheridan Libraries, John Hopkins University; pp. 50 – 51 Tom Liekens / photo by Diego Franssens; p. 52 De Agostini Picture Library / Getty Images; p. 55 Private Collection / Prismatic Pictures / Bridgeman; p. 56 Metropolitan Museum of Art, New York, The Elisha Whittelsey Collection, The Elisha Whittelsey Fund, 1949; pp. 58-59 Bibliothèque Nationale, Paris, France / Bridgeman Images; p. 60 Historia naturalis Brasiliae / Photo © CCI / Bridgeman Images; p. 63 Kunstkammer Georg Laue, Munich/London; p. 64 Natural History Museum, London, UK / Bridgeman Images; pp. 66 – 67 Lukasweb / Collection KMSKA Antwerp; p. 69 Granger / Bridgeman Images; p. 70 Paul Fearn / Alamy Stock Photo; pp. 72 – 73 Tommaso Riva; p. 75 National Geographic Creative / Alamy Stock Photo; p. 76 National Geographic Creative / Alamy Stock Photo; p. 77 National Geographic Creative / Alamy Stock Photo; p. 78 Science Photo Library; p. 79 Collection Fotomuseum Antwerp; p. 80 Classic Collection A17 / Alamy Stock Photo; p. 83 Buffalo Bill Center of the West; pp. 84 – 85 Tom Liekens / photo by Diego Franssens; p. 86 Private Collection / Photo © Christie's Images / Bridgeman Images; p. 89 Finch & Co; pp. 90 – 91 bpk / Kupferstichkabinett, SMB / Dietmar Katz; pp. 92 – 93 Tom Liekens / photo by Diego Franssens; p. 94 KHM-Museumsverband, Vienna; p. 95 Kunstkammer Georg Laue, Munich/London; p. 96 Collection Fotomuseum Antwerp; pp. 98 – 99 Rijksmuseum, Amsterdam; p. 100 University of Amsterdam; p. 102 Hyungkoo Lee; p. 103 Hyungkoo Lee; p. 105 Rijksmuseum, Amsterdam; p. 106 Mauritius Images GmbH / Alamy Stock Photo; p. 108 Royal Zoological Society of Antwerp; p. 110 Private Collection / Archives Charmet / Bridgeman Images; p. 111 Collection KMMA Tervuren / Photo KMMA Tervuren; pp. 112 – 113 Rijksmuseum, Amsterdam; p. 115 John Gould, Australian Museum; p. 117 Rijksmuseum, Amsterdam; p. 119 Finch & Co; p. 120 Kunstkammer Georg Laue, Munich/London; p. 123 Rijksmuseum, Amsterdam; p. 124 Rijksmuseum, Amsterdam; p. 125 Courtesy of Gallery Daxer & Marshall, Munich; p. 126 Metropolitan Museum of Art, New York; p. 128 Private Collection / Bridgeman Images; p. 130 KHM-Museumsverband, Vienna; p. 131 Auction House Millon, Brussels; p. 133 The Royal Danish Library, Copenhagen; p. 134 Rosamond Purcell, with the help of fellow artists and curators; p. 135 Finch & Co; p. 136 Theatrum Mundi Gallery; p. 137 Rijksmuseum, Amsterdam; pp. 138 – 139 Rosamond Purcell, with the help of fellow artists and curators; p. 140 Daniel Horowitz, Rutger Brandt Gallery; pp. 142 – 143 World History Archive / Alamy Stock Photo; p. 145 Chetham's Library, Manchester; pp. 146 – 147 Institut Tessin, Hotel de Marle, Paris, France / Archives Charmet / Bridgeman Images; p. 149 Mitchell Library, State Library of New South Wales, Australia; p. 150 © Angelos bvba / Photo: Pat Verbruggen; pp. 152 – 153 Collection The World of Kina (Ghent) / Photo: Anja Hellebaut; p. 154 Private Collection / Bridgeman Images; p. 155 Daniel Horowitz, Rutger Brandt Gallery; p. 156 Daniel Horowitz, Rutger Brandt Gallery; p. 158 © 2017, VG Bildkunst/Bonn, Photo: Lothar Schnepf, Cologne; p. 160 © The Trustees of the British Museum. All rights reserved; p. 161 © The Elisha Whittelsey Collection, The Elisha Fund, 1953; p. 162 Collection Universiteitsmuseum Utrecht, Photo: Peter Rothengatter, Het FotoAtelier; pp. 164 – 165 Steffen Dam; p. 167 Daniel Horowitz, Rutger Brandt Gallery; pp. 168 – 169 Daniel Horowitz, Rutger Brandt Gallery; p. 171 Private collection / Archives / Bridgeman Images; p. 175 Rijksmuseum, Amsterdam

This book is
MARKED

MARKED is an initiative by Lannoo Publishers

WWW.MARKED-BOOKS.COM

Sign up for our MARKED newsletter with news about new and forthcoming publications on art, interior design, food & travel, photography and fashion as well as exclusive offers and events.

TEXT: Thijs Demeulemeester

TRANSLATION: Lee Preedy

COPY EDITING: Bracha De Man

IMAGE EDITING: Sarah Theerlynck

BOOK DESIGN: Bart Luijten

If you have any questions or comments about the material in this book, please do not hesitate to contact our editorial team: markedteam@lannoo.com

D/2017/45/86 – NUR 640/694
ISBN: 9789401442725
www.lannoo.com